get motiv...

"SUCCESS"

A LIFE THAT IS CLEAN,
A HEART THAT IS TRUE,
AND DOING YOUR BEST.
THAT'S SUCCESS!

get motivated!

Sayings and stories to motivate yourself and others

OWEN COLLINS

HarperCollins*Publishers*

HarperCollins*Publishers*
77–85 Fulham Palace Road, London W6 8JB

First published in Great Britain in 1998 by HarperCollins*Publishers*
1 3 5 7 9 10 8 6 4 2

Compilation copyright © 1998 Owen Collins

Owen Collins asserts the moral right to
be identified as the compiler of this work

A catalogue record for this book
is available from the British Library
ISBN 0 551 03148 4

Printed and bound in Great Britain by
Caledonian International Book Manufacturing, Glasgow

CONDITIONS OF SALE

This book is sold subject to the condition that it
shall not, by way of trade or otherwise, be lent, re-sold,
hired out or otherwise circulated without the publisher's
prior consent in any form of binding or cover other
than that in which it is published and without a
similar condition including this condition being
imposed on the subsequent purchaser.

All rights reserved. No part of this publication may be
reproduced, stored in a retrieval system, or transmitted,
in any form or by any means, electronic, mechanical,
photocopying, recording or otherwise, without the prior
permission of the publishers.

Contents

Introduction — page ix

Part One: Helping Yourself — 1
Know yourself — 2
Getting started — 3
Success — 4
Thinking — 6
Mottos — 8
The inner life — 12
Appreciating beauty — 14
What kind of life are you looking for? — 15
Go placidly — 16
Learning from proverbs — 18
Values — 20
Friendship — 22
Wisdom — 24
Character — 26
A time to reflect — 27
The quest for happiness — 28
Flattery and friendship — 31
Family life — 32
Influences — 34
Relationships — 36
Reflection — 38
Exercise — 40
Change — 41
Ten ways to make yourself ill — 42
Ten *more* ways to make yourself ill! — 44
Personal growth — 46

Part Two: Becoming Motivated — 49
The 'vision' thing — 50
Setting goals — 52
Optimism and pessimism — 55
Excuses, excuses — 56
Achieving — 58
Getting things done — 60

Ambition	62
Winners and losers	64
Learning from heroes and heroines	66
Learning from Benjamin Franklin	68
Recognition	70
Secrets of success	71
Learning from Andrew Carnegie	72
Dreaming	74
Positive attitudes towards oneself	76
Helen Keller	77
Positive attitudes towards learning	78
Self-belief	80
Body language	81
Change yourself	85
Perseverance	86
Prepare and act	89
Making decisions	90

Part Three: Overcoming Problems 91

So you failed!	92
The stress rating scale	94
Stress management	97
The *MotivAider*	101
Greed	103
Fearing fear	105
Beating your fear	107
Pride and prejudice	109
Making mistakes	111
Anger	112
Worry	115
Criticism	117
Revenge and envy	119
Gossip	121
Busyness	122
Overweight and underweight	123

Part Four: Enhancing your Positive Qualities 125
Leadership 126
Enthusiasm 128
Habits 130
Principles 131
Enhance your communications 132
Receiving strength from others 134
Contentment 136
Genius 138
Crying 139
Risk-taking 140
Positive attitudes towards life 142
Determination 145
Hard work and success 146
Listening 148
Failure need not be final 150
Choosing 151
Understanding and surviving 152
Mind over matter 154
Living with hope 156
Patience 157

Part Five: Helping Others 159
Compassion 160
Service 162
Positive attitudes towards others 164
Being a channel of peace 167
Bringing up children 168
Three old-fashioned virtues 170
Being helpful 172
Be an encourager 174
Teamwork 176
Spreading a little happiness 178
Uncommon graces 180
Solving problems 181
Coping with retirement 182
Going to sleep 183
Serving others 184

Learning and teaching	186
Kindness	188
Giving versus getting	190
Showing love	192

Introduction

This book is designed to help *you* – whether you are a rising star, a falling star, whether you are immersed with bringing up a family or happily sailing along in your chosen career.

Like other self-help books this one concentrates on common sense – what some books grandly call *universal wisdom*. But as Voltaire once remarked, '*Le sens commun n'est pas si commun*' (common sense is not so common). Or, as Stephen William has observed, 'The problem with common sense is that it gets overruled by common practice' (*Managing Pressure for Peak Performance*).

'This book is guaranteed to change your life'

'This book is guaranteed to change your life' is the implied or openly stated claim of most self-help books. Here's an example: '*The Power and Peace of Principle-Centered Living* will show how the fourth generation approach will literally transform the quality of your day and the nature of what you do… We are convinced that this material can empower you to close the gap between what's deeply important to you and the way you spend your time' (Stephen Covey and Roger Merrill, *First Things First: to Live, to Love, to Learn, to Leave a Legacy*).

If each '100 ways to transform your life overnight, to superperson' type of book delivered what it claimed, why is there any need for more than one self-help book? I think that part of the answer is that we need to hear different things at different times. What we need to learn to help us this year is likely to be different from what we needed to hear last year. Also we are often helped, not by some great 1000-page book, but by a sound-bite.

There are masses of helpful ideas in the flood of new self-help books published each year. Many of the pages in this book are simply summaries of large and very technical books on topics like body language, stress and motivation.

Some authors of self-help books are hailed as original, innovative writers, but many of them just borrow other people's ideas.

It's been said, 'If you copy from one person, it's plagiarism; if you copy from two people, it's called research'.

Dale Carnegie openly admitted that he used other people's thoughts: 'The ideas I stand for are not mine. I borrowed them from Socrates. I swiped them from Chesterfield. I stole them from Jesus. And I put them in a book.' He made quite a success of this and is perhaps best known for his book *How to Win Friends and Influence People*, which has sold over 10 million copies in 30 languages.

The power of proverbs

Much of the material collected in this book is distilled wisdom in the form of a proverb. Many proverbs can be traced back hundreds, if not thousands of years. The latest 'new' idea I have detected in recently published books is their recommendation to their readers to return to what they call 'Wisdom literature' – simply a reference to the greatest religious and philosophical books ever written. As William James observed, 'To neglect wise sayings of great thinkers is to deny ourselves our truest education.' Winston Churchill was a great proverb addict. He said 'Every man like myself, who never went to college, can largely make up for that lack by reading the wise sayings of the great men of the past, who gladly left their wisdom and experience in proverbs for us who follow them.'

There really is no reason to be reluctant about learning from proverbs. 'Pygmies placed on the shoulders of giants see more than the giants themselves.' Lucan, *Civil War*, 2.10. Samuel Taylor Coleridge expressed the same truth when he wrote, 'The dwarf sees further than the giant, when he has the giant's shoulder to mount on.' The great scientist Isaac Newton also expressed the same idea when he said, 'If I have seen further it is by standing on the shoulders of giants.'

Sources of wisdom

We have to be open to some rather strange sources of wisdom in order to learn how we can help ourselves. So super-models, presidents, monarchs, pop stars, learned philosophical eggheads, literary giants and popular charismatic leaders all rub shoulders in the pages of this book. One great question to ask when reading a book is: 'Do I want to learn from what I read?' If we do we are happy to learn even from those we disagree with. Thus 'It is allowable to learn even from an enemy' (Latin proverb); 'From the errors of others a wise man corrects his own' (Publilius Syrus); 'I make it my rule to lay hold of light and embrace it, though it be held forth by a child or an enemy' (Jonathan Edwards).

The best way to help others is to make sure that you have some wisdom yourself! This book is arranged so that we become wiser and happier people ourselves, using our abilities to their limits. Then we are better able to help others, and the last section of this book *'Helping Others'*, has this as its theme.

Often, the skill in helping other people is knowing what they need reminding of in their present predicament. As Samuel Johnson said, 'People need to be reminded more often than they need to be instructed'.

part one

Helping Yourself

Know yourself

Know thyself.
   Inscription over the entrance to the temple of Apollo at Delphi

Enlightenment

He who knows others is wise; he who knows himself is enlightened.
   Lao Tzu

We hide from ourselves

One's own self is well hidden from one's own self: of all mines and treasures, one's own is the last to be dug up.
   Friedrich Nietzsche

Some objectives in order to know yourself

1. **Grow.**
   Daily grow in wisdom and knowledge.
2. **Think.**
   Time five minutes a day to think about yourself.
3. **Observe.**
   Work out what your strong points are and what your weak points are.
4. **Pursue ideas.**
   Don't just daydream. Follow your ideas through. Act as necessary.

Getting started

By way of introduction

The secret of getting ahead is getting started.
  Sally Berger

Thomas Carlyle was paralysed

Thomas Carlyle did not want to believe his ears. His friend, the philosopher John Stuart Mill, burst into his study to break the news that his manuscript, which he had given him to read the previous night, had just been used to start a fire by the maid.

Carlyle sank into despair, as he knew this was the only copy of his precious manuscript. For weeks he was paralysed and could do no work. One day, as he looked out of the window, he saw some bricklayers at work.

'It came to me,' he wrote later, 'that as they lay brick on brick, so I could still lay word on word, sentence on sentence.'

He started to rewrite *The French Revolution*, which became a 'classic' in his own lifetime.

A fact to ponder

A journey
of a
thousand miles
must begin
with a
single step.
  Lao Tzu

A nugget of wisdom

What you can do, or dream you can, begin it.
Boldness has genius, power and magic in it.
Only engage, and then the mind grows heated;
Begin it and the task will be completed.
  Goethe

Success

Self-help book slogans

1. Think you can succeed and you will.
2. Think victory and you will.
3. Get the action habit.
4. Dream creatively.
5. Magnify your thinking patterns.
6. Think success – don't think failure.
7. Build castles – don't dig graves.
8. Concentrate on important things.
9. Think big.
10. A manager's most valuable resource is people.
11. Think and grow rich.
13. Make every day a success.
14. You are what you think you are.
15. Keep your commitment to your commitment.
16. PMA: have a Positive Mental Attitude.
17. Great achievements come through great struggles.
19. Believe that it can be done.
20. You can do anything you want.
21. You can be anything you want.
22. We move towards what we picture in our mind.

Desire

Desire is half of life. Indifference is half of death.
   Author unknown

Passion

A strong passion for any object will ensure success, for the desire of the end will point out the means.
   William Hazlitt, English essayist

The highest level of personal achievement

A Gallup poll once questioned 250,000 people who had been categorized as 'successful' people. One of the questions was 'When did they achieve the highest level of personal achievement?' The answer given was 'When the strengths of these successful people were lined up with their abilities'.

Failure to plan

Failure to plan is knowingly planning to fail.
   Author unknown

If at first you don't succeed ...

Football coach Vincent Thomas Lombardi (1913–1970), born in New York City, exemplified the drive and determination he instilled in his players. He played college and professional football and coached at high school, college, and professional level. Under his leadership the Green Bay Packers won five national championships in US professional football in the 1960s, dominating the sport.

Football is like life ...

Football is like life – it requires perseverance, self-denial, hard work, sacrifice, dedication and respect for authority.
   Vincent Thomas Lombardi

Success is ...

Success is the ability to go from failure to failure without losing your enthusiasm.
   Winston Churchill

Thinking

Great Minds

Great minds discuss ideas.
Average minds discuss events.
Small minds discuss people.
Author unknown

A closed mind

A closed mind is like a closed book; just a block of wood.
Chinese proverb

We are what we think

We are what we think.
All that we are arises with our thoughts.
With our thoughts we make the world.
Buddha

I trusted my mum

'My doctors told me I would never walk again. My mother told me I would. I believed my mother.'
Wilma Rudolph, three times Olympic gold medal winner. In the 1960 Olympics she won the 100 metres, the 200 metres and was in the winning team of the 4 x 100 metre relay.

You can, too

They
can
because
they
think
they
can.
Virgil

I think, therefore ...

I think, therefore I am.
   René Descartes

Leisure thoughts

The soul is dyed the colour of its leisure thoughts.
   W.R. Inge

Teach people how to think

Our greatest need is to teach people how to think – not what, but how.
   Thomas Edison

Sow a thought

   Sow a thought, reap a word;
   sow a word, reap a deed;
   sow a deed, reap a habit;
   sow a habit, reap a character;
   sow a character, reap a destiny.
   Author unknown

Mottos

DIY mottos

Choose a motto.
Adopt a motto.
Compose your own motto.

Eastern wisdom

Manifest plainness,
Embrace simplicity,
Reduce selfishness,
Have few desires.
Lao Tzu

No absolutely destitute child ever refused admission.
Motto of Dr Barnardo's Homes

To the greater glory of God.
Motto of the Society of Jesus

Be prepared.
Motto of the Scouts

Either learn or depart, there is no third choice here.
Motto of Winchester College

Night is coming.
Motto of Samuel Johnson, Walter Scott and Robert M'Cheyne

To a valiant heart nothing is impossible.
Motto of Henry IV of France

The doctor's job:
to cure occasionally;
to help frequently;
to comfort always.
Motto from an American country doctor's surgery

Have you got any rivers which they say are uncrossable? Have you got any mountains you can't tunnel through? We specialize in the wholly impossible. Doing the job that no man can do.
   Motto of the American engineers

Through struggle to the stars.
   Motto of the Royal Air Force

Let Glasgow flourish by the preaching of the Word.
   Motto of the city of Glasgow

Union makes strength.
   Motto of the King of the Belgians

Go for souls, and go for the worst.
   Motto of William Booth, founder of the Salvation Army

Find a way or make one.
   Motto of Henry Ford

Never speak of others' faults nor your own virtues.
   Motto of Bob Hope

I will go anywhere provided it is forward.
   Motto of David Livingstone, pioneer missionary

I serve.
   Motto of the Prince of Wales since 1346

In God we trust
   'In God we trust' first appeared on US coins after 22 April 1864, when Congress passed an act authorizing the coinage of a 2-cent piece bearing this motto. Thereafter, Congress extended its use to other coins. On 30 July 1956, it became the national motto.

You may be whatever you resolve to be.
   Motto of Thomas J. ('Stonewall') Jackson

Mottos

Make love, not war.
>Motto of student radicals in the 1960s.

Citius, altius, fortius
Faster, higher, stronger.
>Motto of the Olympic Games

American states

Ditat Deus
God enriches.
>Motto of Arizona

Nil sine numine
Nothing without providence.
>Motto of Colorado

Ua Mau Ke Ea O Ka Aina I Ka Pono
The life of the land is perpetuated in righteousness.
>Motto of Hawaii

Ad astra per aspera
To the stars through difficulties.
>Motto of Kansas

Excelsior
Ever upward.
>Motto of New York

With God, all things are possible.
>Motto of Ohio

Labor omnia vincit
Labour conquers all things.
>Motto of Oklahoma

Dum spiro spero
While I breathe, I hope.
Animis opibusque parati
Prepared in mind and resources
    Motto of South Carolina

Friendship.
    Motto of Texas

Industry.
    Motto of Utah

Choose a motto

Choose a motto you like.

Adopt a motto

Adopt a motto for a month.
See if you can live up to it.
Try choosing a different one each month.

Compose your own motto

Write your own motto and see if you can live by it.

The inner life

Greek wisdom

Start with self

Let
him
that
would
move
the
world
first
move
himself.
   Socrates

We must have richness of soul.
   Antiphanes, *Greek Comic Fragments*

If you wish to be good,
first consider that you are wicked.
   Epictetus

Looking within

If we do not quiet our minds, outward comfort will do no more for us than a golden slipper on a gouty foot.
   John Bunyan

If better were within, better would come out.
   Thomas Fuller

The greatest fault is to be conscious of none.
   Thomas Carlyle

A super-model's viewpoint

I love the confidence that make-up gives me.
   Super-model Tyra Banks

Conscience

A good conscience is a soft pillow.
   German proverb

Confession is good for the soul.
   Scottish proverb

Conscience is the perfect interpreter of life.
   Karl Barth

A guilty conscience needs to confess. A work of art is a confession.
   Albert Camus

Conscience is not an infallible guide. Consciences need educating to distinguish between right and wrong.

Sincere ignorance

Nothing in the world is more dangerous than sincere ignorance and conscientious stupidity.
   Martin Luther King

> **Poet's corner**
>
> It takes less time to do a thing right, than it does to explain why you did it wrong.
>   Henry Wadsworth Longfellow

Appreciating beauty

A grain of sand

To see the World in a grain of sand,
And a Heaven in a wild flower,
Hold Infinity in the palm of your hand,
And Eternity in an hour ...
William Blake, *Auguries of Innocence*

Beauty in our hearts

Though we travel the world over to find the beautiful, we must carry it with us or we find it not.
Ralph Waldo Emerson

A gift from God

Beauty is the gift of God.
Aristotle

Divine beauty

The being of all things is derived from the divine beauty.
Thomas Aquinas

Welcome beauty

Beauty is God's handwriting.
Welcome it
in every fair face,
every fair day,
every fair flower.
Charles Kingsley

A joy for ever

A thing of beauty is a joy for ever:
Its loveliness increases; it will never
Pass into nothingness.
John Keats, *Endymion*, l.1

What kind of life are you looking for?

The canvas of life

Life is a great big canvas, and you should throw all the paint on it you can.
    Danny Kaye

Explore, dream, discover

Twenty years from now you will be more disappointed by the things you didn't do than by the ones you did do. So throw off the bowlines. Sail away from the safe harbour. Catch the trade winds in your sails.
    Explore.
    Dream.
    Discover.
    Mark Twain

Miracles

There are only two ways to live your life. One is as though nothing is a miracle. The other is as though everything is a miracle.
    Albert Einstein

Don't 'be yourself'

'Be yourself' is about the worst advice you can give to people.
    Mark Twain

Service and reciprocity

To fulfil basic human needs the principles of service and reciprocity are required.
'What you do not want done to yourself, do not do to others.'
    Confucius

Doing things faster

Doing more things faster is no substitute for doing the right things.

Go placidly

The Desiderata

Go placidly amid the noise and haste and remember what peace there may be in silence.

As far as possible, without surrender, be on good terms with all persons.
Speak your truth quietly and clearly
... and listen to others,
>even the dull and ignorant:
>they too have a story.

Avoid loud and aggressive persons;
>they are vexations to the spirit.

If you compare yourself to others ...
>you may become vain and bitter ...
>for always there will be greater and lesser persons than yourself.

Enjoy your achievements as well as your plans.
Keep interested in your own career:
>however humble ...
>it is a real possession in the changing fortunes of time.

Exercise caution in your business affairs – for the world is full of trickery.
But let this not blind you to what virtue there is ... many persons strive for high ideals and every life is full of heroism.

Be yourself ...
>especially do not feign affection ...
>neither be cynical about love ...

for in the face of all aridity and disenchantment it is as perennial as the grass.
Take kindly the counsel of the years ...
>gracefully surrendering the things of youth.

Nurture strength of spirit to shield you in sudden misfortune.

But do not distress yourself with imaginings …
   many fears are born of fatigue and loneliness.

Beyond wholesome discipline …
   be gentle with yourself.

You are a child of the universe
   – no less than the trees and the stars …
   you have a right to be here.
And whether or not it is clear to you … no doubt the universe is unfolding as it should.

Therefore be at peace with God, whatever you conceive him to be.

And whatever your labours and aspirations in the noisy confusion of life …
   keep peace with your soul –
      with all its sham,
      drudgery and broken dreams …
   it is still a beautiful world.

Be careful.
Strive to be happy.

Learning from proverbs

So says the president

I borrow all I can
I use all the brains I have and borrow all I can from the classics and wise sayings.
   Thomas Woodrow Wilson

Great sayings

Mankind would lose half its wisdom built up over the centuries if it lost its great sayings. They contain the best parts of the best books.
   Thomas Jefferson

The book of proverbs

Any reading is better than none, but I prefer the book of the century rather than the book of the week or any cheap novel. Better still the book of our centuries – the book of Proverbs.
   Theodore Roosevelt

Wise sayings

Wise sayings are like great men talking to us. It's the closest most of us can get to greatness. They are the cheapest teachers, consultants, advisers, guidelines, pilots, signposts, guardians and counsellors.

They make us wise in one hundredth of the time of any other sources of knowledge or wisdom.

Get closely acquainted with them. They're short-cuts to wisdom. Yes, they're just common sense, but common sense ten feet high.

Few young people accept such simple truths as found in them. No glamour, no hocus-pocus, no dramatics, no magic; just old-fashioned words, but power found nowhere else.
   Author unknown

The surest anchors

In this hectic age, when most of us are unsure, confused and troubled, the surest anchors, guides and advisors are the wise sayings of great men of the past.

Clifton Fadiman

The wisdom of the ages

Time has weeded out of the greatest books all the unnecessary details and left us the gist, the essentials – the Proverbs. They are the wisdom of the ages in the fewest words.

Goethe

The priceless advice in proverbs

Fire your ambition and courage by studying the priceless advice in the proverbs and sayings. They're the shortest road to wisdom you'll ever find.

Alexander Graham Bell

Quality not quantity

Proverbs give us quality, not quantity. An hour of reading Proverbs is usually worth weeks, even months or years, of ordinary reading. Here is wisdom, not knowledge.

Montaigne

Read proverbs

Every man like myself, who never went to college, can largely make up for that lack by reading the wise sayings of the great men of the past, who gladly left their wisdom and experience in proverbs for us who follow them.

Winston Churchill

A proverb a day

1. Read a proverb you like first thing in the morning.
2. See if you can put the proverb into practice during your day.
3. Before you go to sleep, evaluate your day. How did you match up to your proverb? How could you do better tomorrow?

Values

What lasts?

Two things are infinite: the universe and human stupidity; and I'm not sure about the universe.
    Albert Einstein

Ourselves

The fault, dear Brutus, is not in our stars, but in ourselves.
    William Shakespeare, *Julius Caesar*, I.ii.134

The heart

It is only
with the heart
that one can see rightly;
what is essential
is invisible
to the eye.
    Antoine de Saint-Exupery

On the inside

What lies behind us and lies before us are small matters compared to what lies within us.
    Ralph Waldo Emerson

But can 50 million people be wrong?

Whenever you find yourself on the side of the majority, it is time to pause and reflect.
    Mark Twain

Advice from a campaigner

Set yourself earnestly to discover what you are made to do, and then give yourself passionately to the doing of it.
    Martin Luther King, Jr

Injustice

Injustice anywhere is a threat to justice everywhere.
Martin Luther King

The Wicked Bible

In 1631 Robert Barker and Martin Lucas, the King's printers in London, printed an edition of the Bible, with numerous mistakes in it. When it came to the seventh commandment, the readers, on the highest authority, were encouraged to commit adultery.

Their version read, 'Thou shalt commit adultery'. This version of the Bible became known as the *Wicked Bible*.

Charles I had all the 1000 published copies recalled and fined the printers £3000.

Dignity

It is only people of small moral stature who have to stand on their dignity.
Arnold Bennett

The dignity of manual work

No race can prosper till it learns that there is as much dignity in tilling a field as in writing a poem.
Booker T. Washington, *Up from Slavery*

Friendship

Take care in choosing friends

Keep away from people who try to belittle your ambitions. Small people always do that, but the really great make you feel that you, too, can become great.
Mark Twain

Hang on to your friends

> So long as we love we serve;
> So long as we are loved by others,
> I would almost say that we are indispensable;
> And no man is useless while he has a friend.
> Robert Louis Stevenson

My friend Franklin

Meeting Franklin Roosevelt was like opening your first bottle of champagne; knowing him was like drinking it.
Winston Churchill

Making friends

The only way to have a friend is to be one.
Ralph Waldo Emerson

Calling at 4 a.m.

It is the friends that you can call at 4 a.m. that matter.
Marlene Dietrich

Friends and happiness

Of all the things which wisdom provides to make us entirely happy, much the greatest is the possession of friendship.
Epicurus

An honest friend

We are all travellers in the wilderness of this world, and the best we can find in our travels is an honest friend.
Robert Louis Stevenson

Friendship is rare

Love is rarer than genius itself. And friendship is rarer than love.
  Charles Peguy, *Basic Verities*

Loneliness

I think I'm the world's loneliest man.
  Michael Jackson, 1988

The glory of friendship

The glory of friendship is not the outstretched hand, nor the kindly smile nor the joy of companionship; it is the spiritual inspiration that comes to one when he discovers that someone else believes in him and is willing to trust him.
  Ralph Waldo Emerson

A second self

A friend is a second self.
  Latin proverb

A true friend

A judicious friend, into whose heart we may pour out our souls, and tell our corruptions as well as our comforts, is a very great privilege.
  George Whitefield

The rich need true friends

Loneliness is the universal problem of rich people.
  Joan Collins

Wisdom

Wisdom is ...

Wisdom is to live in the present, plan for the future, and profit from the past.
   Anonymous

Honesty

Honesty is the first chapter of the book of wisdom.
   Thomas Jefferson

Theoretical and practical wisdom

Theoretical wisdom is insight into the true nature of things and knowing the most appropriate response. Practical wisdom is the ability to apply this in real life.

Great wisdom is ...

> Great wisdom is generous;
> petty wisdom is contentious.
> Great speech is impassioned,
> small speech cantankerous.
>   Chuang Tzu

Wiser today

Never be ashamed to own you have been in the wrong, 'tis but saying you are wiser today than you were yesterday.
   Jonathan Swift

The difference between wisdom and happiness

There is a difference between happiness and wisdom: he that thinks himself the happiest man, really is so; but he that thinks himself the wisest is generally the greatest fool.
   Charles Caleb Colton (1780–1832)

Knowledge and wisdom

Knowledge comes, but wisdom lingers.
   Alfred, Lord Tennyson

Wisdom is the right use of knowledge. To know is not to be wise. Many men know a great deal, and are all the greater fools for it. There is no fool so great as the knowing fool. But to know how to use knowledge is to have wisdom.
   C.H. Spurgeon

> **Poet's corner**
>
> **Knowledge and wisdom**
> Knowledge is proud that he has learned so much;
> wisdom is humble that he knows no more.
>   William Cowper
>
> **Common sense**
> Common sense in an uncommon degree is what the world calls wisdom.
>   Samuel Taylor Coleridge
>
> **A wise man**
> A wise man will make more opportunities than he finds.
>   Francis Bacon

The meaning of our existence?

Being religious means asking passionately the question of the meaning of our existence and being willing to receive answers, even if the answers hurt.
   Paul Tillich

The source of wisdom

Wisdom is knowing the source of wisdom.

Wisdom

Character

In war

In war, three-quarters turns on personal character and relations; the balance of manpower and materials counts only for the remaining quarter.
    Napoleon

I'm so disorganized!

Personal organization is a universal struggle. Internal organization is the most difficult thing in the world to master.

German philosopher

Men best show their character in trifles, where they are not on their guard. It is in the insignificant matters, and in the simplest habits, that we often see the boundless egotism which pays no regard to the feelings of others, and denies nothing to itself.
    Arthur Schopenhauer

Fame, popularity and money

Fame is a vapour, popularity is an accident, and money takes wings. The only thing that endures is character.
    O.J. Simpson

The difference between reputation and character

Reputation is what people think you are. Character is the real you – who you really are.
Reputation is valuable; but character is priceless.

Fame and virtue

The thirst for fame is greater than for virtue.
    Latin proverb

A time to reflect

Creative solitude

One of the greatest necessities in America is to discover creative solitude.
    Carl Sandburg

Waiting

The man who goes alone can start today; but he who travels with another must wait till that other is ready.
    Henry David Thoreau

How to read

To read without reflecting is like eating without digesting.
    Edmund Burke

Taking time to reflect

By taking time to reflect on life, instead of spending all our time just living, we can become aware of the consequences of our choices and learn from living.

Springs of life

Watch over your heart with all diligence, for from it flow the springs of life.
    Proverbs 4:23

Reflect on your present blessings

Reflect on your present blessings, of which every man has many, not on your past misfortunes, of which all men have some.
    Charles Dickens

The quest for happiness

Storybook happiness

Storybook happiness involves every form of pleasant thumb-twiddling; true happiness involves the full use of one's powers and talents.

    John W. Gardner, President of the Carnegie Foundation

Peace comes from …

Peace
comes
from
within.
Do
not
seek
it
without.
Buddha

Millions bring no happiness

I have made many millions, but they have brought me no happiness. I would barter them all for the days I sat on an office stool in Cleveland and counted myself rich on three dollars a week.

    John D. Rockefeller

The recipe for happiness

If
you
want
to
be
happy,
be.
Leo Tolstoy, *Kosma Prutkov*

Helping yourself

Complete happiness

Complete happiness is knowing God.
   John Calvin

> ### So says the president
> #### Tranquillity
> It is neither wealth nor splendour, but tranquillity and occupation, which gives happiness.
>   Thomas Jefferson

Happiness is ...

Happiness is good health and a bad memory.
   Ingrid Bergman

Bequeathing happiness

By being happy we sow anonymous benefits upon the world.
   Robert Louis Stevenson

Cheerfulness and contentment

Cheerfulness and contentment are great beautifiers, and are famous preservers of good looks.
   Charles Dickens

The scholar and the poor man

On his way to church, a scholar was surprised to see a man in tattered clothes and barefoot. Nevertheless, as a good Christian, he greeted the poor man: 'May God give you a good morning!'
   The poor man replied cheerfully, 'I have never yet had a bad morning.'
   'Then may God give you good luck!'
   'I have never yet had bad luck.'
   'Well, may God give you happiness!'
   'I have never yet been unhappy.'
   The scholar then asked the man, 'Could you please explain yourself to me? I do not understand.'
   And the poor man replied, 'With pleasure! You wish me a

The quest for happiness

good morning, yet I have never had a bad morning. For when I am hungry, I praise God; when I feel cold, or when it is raining or snowing, I praise God; and that is why I have never had a bad morning.

'You wish that God may give me luck. However, I have never had bad luck. This is because I live with God and always feel what he does for me is the best. Whatever God sends me, be it pleasant or unpleasant, I accept with a grateful heart. That is why I have never had bad luck.

'Finally, you wish that God should make me happy. But I have never been unhappy. For all I desire is to follow God's will; I have surrendered my will so totally to God's will that, whatever God wants, that is what I also want.

'That is why I have never been unhappy.'
Meister Eckhart

Three essentials

Three grand essentials to happiness in this life are:
    something to do,
        something to love,
            and something to hope for.
Joseph Addison

Be happy while you can

Be happy while you're living, for you're a long time dead.
Scottish proverb

Flattery and friendship

Flattery and friendship

What really flatters a man is that you think him worth flattering.
   George Bernard Shaw

I can't be your friend, and your flatterer too.
   Thomas Fuller, *Gnomologia*

A man's body is remarkably sensitive. Pat him on the back and his head swells.
   La Rochefoucauld

Flattery corrupts both the receiver and giver.
   Edmund Burke

Friends who will not flatter

God send me a friend that will tell me of my faults.
A faithful friend is an image of God.
   French proverbs

Aesop's fables

A fox and a raven

A certain fox spotted a raven in a tree with a morsel in his mouth, which started his mouth watering. The problem was how to obtain the morsel. 'Oh blessed bird,' said the fox, 'the delight of gods and men.' The fox continued to extol all the virtues of the raven, his graceful ways, his beautiful plumage and his gift of being able to predict the future. 'And now,' said the fox, 'if you had a voice to match your other excellent qualities, the sun in the heavens could not show the world a creature to match you.'

This sickly flattery immediately made the raven want to give the fox an example of his singing. But as he opened his mouth to sing he dropped his breakfast, which the fox gobbled up. The fox then told the raven to remember that whatever he had said about his beauty, he had said nothing about his brains.

Family life

Francis Bacon's wish

If I wasn't a painter I wish I was a mother.
   Francis Bacon

Like father, like son

Telling lies and showing off to get attention are mistakes I made that I don't want my kids to make.
   Jane Fonda

Example

Example is not the main thing in influencing others.
It is the only thing.
   Albert Schweitzer

Bringing up a family

Perhaps the greatest social service that can be rendered by anybody to the country and to mankind is to bring up a family.
   George Bernard Shaw

A few minutes of your time

The best inheritance a parent can give his children is a few minutes of his time each day.

Your presence

Your children need your presence more than your presents.
   Jesse Jackson

Keeping good company

The soul is healed by being with children.
   Fyodor Dostoyevsky

Seeing love

The best training a father can give his children is to love their mother.
　　Author unknown

Follow your instinct

What good mothers and fathers instinctively feel like doing for their babies is usually best after all.
　　Benjamin Spock

Americans obey their children

The thing that impresses me most about America is the way parents obey their children.
　　Duke of Windsor

God made mothers

God could not be everywhere and therefore he made mothers.
　　Jewish proverb

We owe everything to our mum

Men are what their mothers made them.

Influences

Early influences

If a child lives with criticism,
he learns to condemn.
If a child lives with hostility,
he learns to fight.
If a child lives with fear,
he learns to be apprehensive.
If a child lives with pity,
he learns to feel sorry for himself.
If a child lives with jealousy,
he learns to feel guilty.
If a child lives with encouragement,
he learns to be self-confident.
If a child lives with tolerance,
he learns to patient.
If a child lives with praise,
he learns to be appreciative.
If a child lives with acceptance,
he learns to love.
If a child lives with approval,
he learns to like himself.
If a child lives with recognition,
he learns to have a goal.
If a child lives with fairness,
he learns what justice is.
If a child lives with honesty,
he learns what truth is.
If a child lives with sincerity,
he learns to have faith in himself and
those around him.
If a child lives with love,
he learns that the world is
a wonderful place to live in.

Author unknown

None of us lives unto himself or herself

We all influence other people for good or bad each day.
We are all influenced by others every day.

The impact of change

Change has considerable psychological impact on the human mind.

> To the fearful
>   it is threatening
>   because it means that things may get worse.
> To the hopeful
>   it is encouraging
>   because things may get better.
> To the confident
>   it is inspiring
>   because the challenge exists to make things better.

Obviously, then, one's character and frame of mind determine how readily he brings about change and how he reacts to change that is imposed on him.
   King Whitney Jr, President of Personnel Laboratory Inc.

The strongest influences

The strongest influences in my life and my work are always whomever I love. Whomever I love and am with most of the time, or whomever I *remember* most vividly. I think that's true of everyone, don't you?
   Tennessee Williams

Tommy's trombone

The thing that influenced me most was the way Tommy played his trombone.
   Frank Sinatra

Influences

Relationships

A definition

Relationships have been defined as hitting it off – especially with those we don't like!

One to one is hard

The easiest kind of relationship for me is with ten thousand people. The hardest is with one.
    Joan Baez

To ponder

> ### Some sayings to choose from, to help us get along with other people
>
> If a man be gracious and courteous to strangers, it shows he is a citizen of the world.
>   Francis Bacon, *Essays*, 'Of Goodness'
>
> A man's feeling of good will *toward* others is the strongest magnet for drawing good will *from* others.
>   Chesterfield
>
> We are interested in others if they are interested in us.
>   Horace
>
> If you want people to be glad to meet you, you must be glad to meet them – and show it.
>   Goethe
>
> Use your head to handle yourself, your heart to handle others.
>   Author unknown
>
> You can never establish a personal relationship without opening up your own heart.
>   Paul Tournier
>
> Charm may in seven words be found: forget yourself and think of those around.
>   Author unknown

Measured advice from 'Bulldog' Sir Winston Churchill

I have no secret. You haven't learned life's lesson very well if you haven't noticed that you can give the tone or colour, or decide the reaction you want of people in advance.

It's unbelievably simple.

> If you want them to take an interest in you, take an interest in them first.
>
> If you want to make them nervous, become nervous yourself.
>
> If you want them to shout and raise their voices, raise yours and shout.
>
> If you want them to strike you, strike first.

It's as simple as that. People will treat you like you treat them. It's no secret. Look about you. You can prove it with the next person you meet.

The golden rule

The law that governs quality in our relationships with others stems from the Golden Rule and has been called the law of reciprocity. In essence it states: Life is better when we treat others as we would be treated.

Do as you would be done by

Do as you would be done by is the surest method that I know of pleasing.

Chesterfield, *Letters*, 16 October 1747

Concluding thought

Do unto others as you would have them do to you.

Luke 6:31

Reflection

Learning wisdom

By three methods we may learn wisdom:
   first, by reflection, which is noblest;
   second, by imitation, which is easiest;
   and third by experience, which is the bitterest.
   Confucius

Reflection

   Things worth remembering:
   The value of time.
   The success of perseverence.
   The pleasure of working.
   The dignity of simplicity.
   The worth of character.
   The improvement of talent.
   The influence of example.
   The obligation of duty.
   The wisdom of economy.
   The virtue of patience.
   The joy of originating.
   The power of darkness.
   Author unknown

Sitting quietly each day

All the troubles of life come upon us because we refuse to sit quietly for a while each day in our rooms.
   Blaise Pascal

Take time to ...

   Take time to think:
      it is the course of power.
   Take time to play:
      it is the secret of perpetual youth.
   Take time to read:
      it is the fountain of wisdom.

Take time to pray:
    it is the greatest power on earth.
Take time to laugh:
    it is the music of the soul.
Take time to give:
    it is too short a day to be selfish.
Author unknown

I asked God for ...

I asked God for strength that I might achieve;
I was made weak that I might learn humbly to obey.
I asked for help that I might do greater things;
I was given infirmity that I might do better things.
I asked for riches that I might be happy;
I was given poverty that I might be wise.
I asked for all things that I might enjoy life;
I was given life that I might enjoy all things.
I was given nothing I asked for;
But everything that I had hoped for.
Despite myself, my prayers were answered;
I am among all men most richly blessed.
An unknown Confederate soldier

Exercise

Learn to value physical fitness

Learn to value physical fitness as a means to relaxation and antidote to stress.

Exercise routines

A simple routine constructed round 'clench-and-let-go' exercises can be very effective for releasing stress in a variety of everyday situations.

These exercises work by what is called 'reciprocal innovation': voluntary muscular contraction is followed by relaxation.

1. Sit quietly, eyes closed. Clench both fists and hold them clenched for 15 seconds.
   Then relax and feel the tension drain away from your arm muscles. Repeat this twice.
2. Hunch your shoulders for 15 seconds, bringing them right up towards your ears.
   Now relax. Then repeat twice.
3. Smile as widely as you can, trying to make the smile stretch right across your face: hold the smile for 15 seconds, then relax.
   Repeat this twice.
4. Push your eyebrows so that you look really surprised. Hold, then relax.
   Repeat this twice.
5. Screw up your eyes as tightly as you can, then relax.
   Repeat this twice.

Change

Do you need to change?

Through pride we are ever deceiving ourselves. But deep down below the surface of the average conscience a still, small voice says to us, 'Something is out of tune'.
  Carl Jung

Managing change

Change is a threat or an opportunity. It all depends on how you look at it. A 1994 MORI poll showed that 99% of *The Times* 1000 companies are going through a major change.

Become the change

We must become the change we seek in the world.
  Gandhi

Act as if you already had it

Often called the father of American psychology, William James said, 'If you want a quality, act as if you already had it.'

Assume a virtue

Assume a virtue, if you have it not.
  William Shakespeare, *Hamlet* III.iv.160

Take stock

Make a list of the things that you are proud to have done. It does not matter how important or trivial the things are. Include them all.

DIY character analysis

Take a piece of paper and make three columns. In the first column list all your strengths and good qualities. In the second column list all your weaknesses and bad qualities. In the third column list alternatives you would like to possess to your own weaknesses and bad qualities.

Ten ways to make yourself ill

1. Spend your life concentrating on the wrong things

Most people fail in life because they major in minor things.

2. Be a slave to fashion

Fashion takes many forms, such as what it is fashionable to do and how we should think about the world. In this, fashion is not confined to clothes.

Fashion wears out
The fashion wears out more apparel than the man.
   William Shakespeare

Copying others
We forfeit three-fourths of ourselves in order to be like other people.
   Arthur Schopenhauer

Following fashion
I cannot and will not cut my conscience to fit this year's fashions.
   Lillian Hellman

Mini-skirts
Never in the history of fashion has so little material been raised so high to reveal so much that needs to be covered so badly.
   Cecil Beaton

3. Ignore basic human needs

There are universal human needs, and nothing works well very long in the human experience that ignores them.

4. Never put up a fight
Never give way to melancholy; resist it steadily, for the habit will encroach.
   Sydney Smith

5. Pleasing people
If we want to feel truly confident, we must break the habit of trying to please all the people, all the time.

6. Putting yourself down
Cut out from your vocabulary such phrases as 'I'm hopeless at …'.

7. Never swap good news

8. Never accept what can't be changed

9. Never have any time for leisure
Leisure is the mother of philosophy.
   Thomas Hobbes

Don't be so busy that you have no leisure
Neither in your actions be sluggish, nor in your conversation without method, nor wandering in your thoughts, nor let there be inward contention in your soul, nor be so busy in life as to have no leisure.
   Marcus Aurelius

10. Never grieve or mourn
Silent sorrow
Silent sorrow is only the more fatal.
   Racine

Ten more ways to make yourself ill!

1. Always be in a hurry

Hurry is not of the devil. It is the devil.
   Carl Jung

This perpetual hurry of business and company ruins me in soul if not in body.
   William Wilberforce

2. Always take yourself very seriously
A tip from a perfectionist
Take your work seriously, but never yourself.
   Dame Margot Fonteyn

Laugh at yourself
You grow up the day you have your first real laugh, at yourself.
   Ethel Barrymore

3. Never say 'no'
Taking on too much
He who undertakes too much seldom succeeds.
   Dutch Proverb

4. Don't live in the present
The present, the past and the future
Every man's life lies within the present; for the past is spent and done with, and the future is uncertain.
   Marcus Aurelius

5. Always indulge in self-pity
Self-pity is not the same as depression. If you are depressed, consult your doctor.

> **Some symptoms of depression**
> 1. Feeling worthless.
> 2. Lack of interest in normal activities.
> 3. Frequent crying.
> 4. Loss of appetite.
> 5. Mood swings.

6. Never get started

The right moment for starting on your next job is not tomorrow or next week; it is *instanter*, or in the American idiom, *right now*.
   Arnold Toynbee

An evangelist's prayer
Lord, help me to begin to begin.
   George Whitefield

7. Insist on being liked by everyone

8. Never allow enough time to arrive comfortably for your next appointment

This will ensure that everyone knows how busy you are.

9. Don't slow down

When your doctor tells you to slow down, throw out the quote: 'I'd rather wear out than rust out.'

10. Make it your civic duty to ...

Make it your civic duty to sit on as many committees as possible. Try to ensure that you are chairperson of them all!

Ten *more* ways to make yourself ill!

Personal growth

The formula

First say to yourself what you would be, then do what you have to do.
   Epictetus

Eastern wisdom
Light in the soul

If there is light in the soul, there will be beauty in the person.
If there is beauty in the person, there will be harmony in the house.
If there is harmony in the house, there will be order in the nation.
If there is order in the nation, there will be peace in the world.
Chinese proverb

Don't continue to be yourself

Don't be yourself. Be superior to the fellow you were yesterday.
   Author unknown

You're not very smart if you're not a little kinder and wiser than yesterday.
   Abraham Lincoln

To put the world in order

To put the world in order,
   we must first put the nation in order;
to put the nation in order,
   we must first put the family in order;
to put the family in order,
   we must cultivate our personal life;
and to cultivate our personal life,
   we must set our hearts right.
Confucius

Helping yourself

A closed mind

A closed mind is like a closed book; just a block of wood.
    Chinese proverb

Shun small defects

If you do not shun small defects, bit by bit you will fall into greater ones.
    Thomas à Kempis

Be kind to yourself

When you cannot get a compliment any other way, pay yourself one.
    Mark Twain

Respect yourself

If you want to be respected, you must respect yourself.
    Spanish proverb

Don't put yourself down

If you really put a small value upon yourself, rest assured that the world will not raise your price.
    Anonymous

Review your life so far

Write down significant events in your life, going back as far as you can remember. At each significant event note if you were powerful or powerless; comfortable or uncomfortable; controlled by others or controlling others.

Make time for yourself

Set time aside, even if it's only a few minutes each day, for yourself. Be quiet. Think about who you are and who you want to be.

part two

Becoming Motivated

The 'vision' thing

The stars

Keep your eyes on the stars, and your feet on the ground.
Theodore Roosevelt

The doughnut

> As you travel on through life,
> Whatever be your goal,
> Keep your eye upon the doughnut
> And not upon the hole.
> **Author unknown**

From the psychiatrist's chair

Look inside

Your vision will become clear only when you can look into your heart.
Who looks outside,
dreams,
who looks inside,
awakes.
   Carl Jung

Skill and imagination

Skill without imagination is craftsmanship and gives us many useful objects such as wickerwork picnic baskets.
   Imagination without skill gives us modern art.
   Tom Stoppard

Einstein and fantasy

When I examine myself and my methods of thought, I come to the conclusion that the gift of fantasy has meant more to me than my talent for absorbing positive knowledge.
Albert Einstein

Imagination

Imagination is the beginning of creation.
   You imagine what you desire,
      you will what you imagine
         and at last you create what you will.
   George Bernard Shaw

Questions to clarify your vision

The best way to maximize the usefulness of the following type of questions is to write down your answers in a book.

1. What's most important to you?
2. What gives your life meaning?
3. What do you want to be?
4. What do you want to do in your life?
5. What is right for you now?
6. What do you need to help you progress this year?

An opera begins ...

An opera begins long before the curtain goes up and ends long after it has come down. It starts in my imagination, it becomes my life, and it stays part of my life long after I've left the opera house.
   Maria Callas

Concluding thought

Imagination is more important than knowledge.
   Albert Einstein

Setting goals

From the psychiatrist's chair

When goal goes,
meaning goes;
when meaning goes,
purpose goes;
when purpose goes,
life goes dead on our hands.
  Carl Jung

Attached or unattached?

People are like buttons:unattached, useless;
attached, indispensable.
People, unattached to a goal, useless.
Attached, men with missions.
  Author unknown

Three rational questions

1. Where am I?
2. Where do I want to be?
3. How do I know I am getting there?
   Author unknown

A fact to ponder

The fool wanders: the wise man travels.
  Thomas Fuller, *Gnomologia*

Scoring goals

Before you score, you must have a goal.
  Author unknown

If you aim at nothing, you will hit it.
  Author unknown

Write it down

Strange as it may seem, a written-down goal tends to attract every ingredient it needs to realize it.
   Author unknown

Aimless Americans

Ninety-five per cent of working American males have no goals in their life.
   Owen Hendrix

How to set realistic goals

Create a master list of things you want.
A quick way to do this is to write down the answer to this question: 'If I had all the money I wanted, and all the opportunities in the world open to me I would ...'

Two questionnaires

The following two questionnaires will help you develop your self-understanding about what your goals in life are.

A: Long-term desires

(a) What do you hope to achieve in your lifetime?
(b) What single thing would make you most happy?
(c) What do you daydream about most often?
(d) Rank the following items, from 1 to 5, in the order of their importance to you:
   - making lots of money
   - being well known
   - doing what you enjoy
   - sharing friendship
   - making a difference through your work.
(e) What do you want very much, but fear going after?
(f) What is the main goal in your life?
(g) What are some other important goals in your life?

B: Short-term desires
(a) What do you want most right now?
(b) What do you want/need in next 24 hours/week/month?
(c) What do you want to own?
(d) What do you want to experience?

Find out what you really want/need

Most people set their goals too low.

Two messages from self-help books:

If you know in your heart and soul what you want, you *can* succeed.

Never underestimate the power of setting goals.

Optimism and pessimism

Are you an optimist or a pessimist?

A pessimist defines a window as something that gets dirty and needs washing.
An optimist defines a window as something to let the light shine through.

A pessimist says a bottle of wine is half empty.
An optimist says a bottle of wine is half full.

The pessimist complains about the wind.
The optimist expects it to change.

The realist adjusts the sails.
    William Arthur Ward

An optimist is a person who sees a green light everywhere, while the pessimist sees only the red spotlight.
The truly wise person is colour-blind.
    Albert Schweitzer

The optimist sees the doughnut but the pessimist sees the hole.

A pessimist sees the difficulty in every opportunity; an optimist sees the opportunity in every difficulty.
    Winston Churchill

Pessimism is an investment in nothing;
optimism is an investment in hope.
    Author unknown

Excuses, excuses

The first most common excuse: 'I would, but my health is not up to it.'

According to Dr Schindler three out of four hospital beds are occupied with people suffering from EII – Emotionally Induced Illness.

How to beat the 'bad health' excuse

1. Don't be talking about your health all the time.
2. Don't worry about your health all the time.
3. Be glad that your health is as good as it is.
4. Repeat to yourself: 'I'd rather wear out than rust out.'

The second most common excuse: 'I would – but I don't have the brains.'

This arises because we underestimate our own intelligence, and also because we confuse intelligence with knowing a mass of facts.

How to beat the 'no brains' excuse

1. Remember: enthusiasm counts for more than a high IQ.
   A person with a low IQ or an average IQ and enthusiasm will go much further than a person with a high IQ who has little or no enthusiasm.
2. 95% of ability boils down to stick-ability.
3. Remind yourself: attitude is more important than intelligence. About 50% of college students in America never complete their courses. Why? It's not a question that they don't have the brains, because they would not have gained a place at the college in the first place if that was in doubt. They 'drop out' through attitude problems – problems with their lecturers, problems with their fellow students.

[Today's students] can put dope in their veins or hope in their brains.
If they can conceive it and believe it, they can achieve it.

They must know it is not their aptitude but their attitude that will determine their altitude.
   Jesse Jackson

4. Remember: thinking is more important than knowing facts.

The third most common excuse: 'I would, but my age is against me'

(A) 'I'm too old'
Winston Churchill and Queen Victoria both became accomplished artists. Neither of them sketched or painted before they were 50 years old.

You are younger today than you ever will be again. Make use of it.
   Anonymous

(B) 'I'm too young'
To exclude from positions of trust and command all those below the age of 44 would have kept Jefferson from writing the Declaration of Independence, Washington from commanding the Continental Army, Madison from fathering the Constitution, Hamilton from serving as secretary of the treasury, Clay from being elected speaker of the House and Christopher Columbus from discovering America.
   John F. Kennedy

How to beat the 'my age' excuse

1. Young and old age are only a liability if you let yourself think that way.
2. Don't say, 'I wish I'd started this earlier in my life.' Make a start now.

Achieving

Work – there's no substitute for it!

Laziness may appear attractive, but work gives satisfaction.
  Anne Frank

An open door

When one door of happiness closes, another opens; but often we look so long at the closed door that we do not see the one that has opened for us.
  Helen Keller

Will-power

Do one thing every day for no other reason than that you don't feel like doing it; the will is the man. Will makes giants.
  William James

An ounce of will-power is worth a pound of learning.
  Nicholas Butler, President of Columbia University

Too many develop every talent except the most vital one of all, the talent to use their talents ... will-power.
  Francis Bacon

Aesop's fables

Slow but sure

A tortoise and a hare had an argument about which of them was the faster and before they separated they agreed to settle the matter at a particular place at a particular time. The hare was so confident about how fast he could run that he gave no thought about the race he had agreed to beat the tortoise in. The hare just lay down in a field and went to sleep. The tortoise was so conscious about his slow speed that he kept on going, and did not even stop when he saw the sleeping hare, until he won the race.

Moral: A naturally gifted person, who does not apply himself to a task, is often beaten by a plodder.

Inch by inch
> Yard by yard, all tasks are hard.
> Inch by inch, they're all a clinch.
> Author unknown

Americans are achievers.
Americans are achievers. They are obsessed with records of achievement in sports and they keep business achievement charts on their office walls and sports awards displayed in their homes.

Churchill's greatest achievement
My most brilliant achievement was my ability to be able to persuade my wife to marry me.
   Winston Churchill

Harmony
Jung held that the most significant task for any person was to achieve harmony between the conscious and the unconscious.

Getting things done

By way of introduction

Good intentions are not enough.
A good start does not ensure a strong finish.
A decision to start a job is 5% of the work.
Following through the decision to start is 95% of the work.

Do it yourself

Do not wait for leaders; do it alone, person to person.
   Mother Teresa

Good intentions are not enough

No one would remember the Good Samaritan if he'd only had good intentions – he had money, too.
   Margaret Thatcher

Little strokes

Little strokes fell great oaks.
   Proverb

Idleness

I don't think necessity is the mother of invention. Invention, in my opinion, arises directly from idleness, possibly also from laziness – to save oneself trouble.
   Agatha Christie

A lazy person is as bad as someone who is destructive.
   Proverbs 12:24

Idleness is the mother of want.
   Greek proverb

Procrastination

When, as a child, I laughed and wept,
  Time crept.
When, as a youth, I dreamed and talked,
  Time walked.
When I became a full-grown man,
  Time ran.
And later, as I older grew,
  Time flew.
Soon I shall find, while travelling on,
  Time gone.
Will Christ have saved my soul by then?
  Amen.
Inscription on clock in Chester Cathedral

Will-power and great talent

There is no such thing as a great talent without great will-power.
  Honoré de Balzac, *La Muse du Département*

Concluding thought

There must be a beginning
of any great matter,
but the continuing
unto the end
until it be thoroughly finished
yields the true glory.
  Francis Drake to Francis Walsingham, 17 May 1587

Ambition

Reach for the stars

Ah, but a man's reach should exceed his grasp, or what's a heaven for?
Robert Browning

Hitch your wagon to a star.
Ralph Waldo Emerson, *Society and Solitude*

The wish

The wish is father to the thought.
Latin proverb

The difference between success and failure

The longer I live, the stronger becomes my conviction that the truest difference
    between success and failure,
    between the strong and the weak,
    between the big and the small man,
    that separates the boys from the men,
is nothing but
        a powerful aim in life
        a purpose once fixed and then death or victory.
  And
        no perfect speech or manners,
        no culture or education,
        no pull or influence,
can make a two-legged creature a man without it.
Thomas Buxton

Love and ambition

    Love's the frailty of the mind,
    When 'tis not with ambition join'd.
    William Congreve, *The Way of the World*

The downside of ambition

Ambition can creep as well as soar.
    Edmund Burke

Love and meekness, lord,
Become a churchman better than ambition.
    William Shakespeare, *Henry VIII*, V.iii

Cromwell, I charge thee, fling away ambition:
By that sin fell the angels. How can man then,
The image of his maker, hope to win by it?
    William Shakespeare, *Henry VIII*, III.ii

Ambition destroys its possessor.
    The Talmud

Today a king, tomorrow nothing.
    French proverb

Today a man, tomorrow a mouse.
    English proverb

> ### From the psychiatrist's chair
> **Being great**
> The strongest want in human nature is the desire to be great.
>   Sigmund Freud

May I ...

May I be no man's enemy, and may I be the friend of that which is eternal and abides.
May I never quarrel with those nearest to me; and if I do, may I be reconciled quickly.
May I love, seek, and attain only what is good.
May I wish for all men's happiness and envy no one.
May I never rejoice in the ill fortune of someone who has wronged me.
May I win no victory that harms either me or my opponent.
    Eusebius

Winners and losers

Activity mistaken for accomplishment

Losers mistake activity for accomplishment.
Winners know that accomplishment is the result of activity.

Winners always have goals

It is my ambition to say in ten sentences what others say in a whole book.
   Friedrich Nietzsche

Winners are not scared of hard work

The harder you work, the luckier you get.
   Gary Player

Winners learn from others

Always imitate the behaviour of winners when you lose.
   Anonymous

Winners don't fear losing

A winner is not afraid to lose.
A loser is secretly afraid of winning.

Losers make no plans

A man who does not plan long ahead will find trouble right at his door.
   Confucius

Worry or concern

There is a great difference between worry and concern.
Worry frets about a problem.
Concern solves a problem.
Winners show concern.
Losers merely fret.

Measure yourself

A valuable measure of success or failure is whether the tough problem you are facing is the same problem you had a year ago.

Just to survive is often a great achievement

Pro football is like nuclear warfare.
There are no winners, only survivors.
    Frank Gifford, New York Giants halfback

Three steps to being a loser

1. Always take time to explain why you lost.
2. Devote your life to thinking about what you might possibly do.
3. Never enjoy what you are doing.

Winners are ...

Winners are ordinary people with extraordinary determination.

How to make a winner

Praise often turns losers into winners.
    Author unknown

Learning from heroes and heroines

An example or a warning?
Aristotle is rightly regarded as a fount of wisdom, but we don't have to agree with *everything* he said.

Let there be a law that no deformed child shall be reared.
   Aristotle, *Politics* 7.14.10

The hero of Africa?
I am the hero of Africa.
   Idi Amin, while President of Uganda

Nobody gets it right all the time
No mortal is wise at all times.
   Pliny

A mixture
Nobody is so bad that he has no good in him.
Nobody is so good that he has no bad in him.

Hero worship
If you try to emulate the good traits of someone you admire you may be accused of hero worship. But you could be accused of many worse things. What's so bad about hero worshipping after all, if your character is built up as a result?

So says the president

Learning from people
Study men, not historians.
   Harry S. Truman

No great man lives in vain

No great man lives in vain.
The history of the world is but the biography of great men.
    Thomas Carlyle, *Heroes and Hero Worship*

> **Poet's corner**
>
> Lives of great men all remind us
> We can make our lives sublime,
> And, departing, leave behind us
> Footprints on the sands of time.
>   **Henry Wadsworth Longfellow, 'A Psalm of Life'**

Learning from Mum

I learned more about Christianity from my mother than from all the theologians in England.
    John Wesley

You have omitted to mention the greatest of my teachers – my mother.
    Winston Churchill, when he was asked to check a list of people who had taught him.

It is impossible that the son of these tears should perish.
    Augustine of Hippo, *Confessions* **(referring to his Christian mother who wept and prayed for him during his years of reckless living).**

No man is poor who has a godly mother.
    Abraham Lincoln

Learning from Benjamin Franklin

Benjamin Franklin (1706–1790), born in Boston, Massachusetts, was an American author, printer, inventor, scientist, publisher and diplomat. He was truly a man of many talents. Franklin was known for his wit and humour, much of which was published in *Poor Richard's Almanac*, and for his proof that lightning was a form of electricity by experimenting with a kite in a thunderstorm. He played a pivotal role in the revolutionary and formative years of the United States. He helped draft the Declaration of Independence in 1776, represented the USA in France during the war, and was involved in negotiating the peace with Britain in 1781. He was a stabilizing figure at the Constitutional Convention in 1787. Franklin founded the world's first public fire department, the first public lending library, and what later became the University of Pennsylvania.

Who is wise?

Who is wise?
    He that learns from everyone.
Who is powerful?
    He that governs his passions.
Who is rich?
    He who is content.
Who is that?
    Nobody.

If you would be loved

If you would be loved, love and be lovable.

Taking life's opportunities

Human felicity is produced not so much by great pieces of good fortune that seldom happen as by little advantages that occur every day.

Anger

Anger is never without a reason but seldom a good one.

Who is strong?

Who is strong?
He that can conquer his bad habits.
   Poor Richard's Almanac, 1744

A little neglect

A little neglect may breed mischief.
   For want of a nail, the shoe was lost;
   for want of a shoe the horse was lost;
   and for want of a horse the rider was lost.
   Poor Richard's Almanac, 1858

A good conscience

A good conscience is a continual Christmas.

Recognition

How to accomplish much

You can accomplish much if you don't care who gets the credit.
　Ronald Reagan

The need to be heard

Sometimes when I sit down to practise and there is no one else in the room, I have to stifle an impulse to ring for the elevator man and offer him money to come in and hear me.
　Artur Rubinstein

General Electric

General Electric (USA) conducted a survey in their offices and laboratories to find out the answer to the question: What motivates our research staff?

To their surprise the answer was not working conditions, salary or promotion prospects. They found that 'recognition' headed the list.

They saw that when someone had accomplished something he/she wanted it recognized.

They realized that recognition is one of the most powerful motivators at work.

More than anything else

More than anything else, people want to be noticed, recognized.
　Goethe

A deep need

The deepest principle in human nature is the craving to be appreciated.
　William James

Secrets of success

Take a chance

Take a chance! All life is a chance. The man who goes farthest is generally the one who is willing to do and dare.
  Dale Carnegie

To invent

To invent, you need a good imagination and a pile of junk.
  Thomas Edison

Business success

The secret of business is to know something nobody else knows.
  Aristotle Onassis

This is to have succeeded

  To laugh often and much;
  to win the respect of intelligent people and the
  affection of children;
  to earn the appreciation of honest critics and
  endure the betrayal of false friends;
  to appreciate beauty;
  to find the best in others;
  to leave the world a bit better,
    whether by a healthy child,
    a garden patch
    or a redeemed social condition;
  to know even one life has breathed easier because you have lived.
  This is to have succeeded.
  Ralph Waldo Emerson

Learning from Andrew Carnegie

An entrepreneur and a philanthropist

Andrew Carnegie (1835–1919), industrialist and philanthropist, had an awesome power in gaining wealth and giving it away. In his thirties, Carnegie made money in stocks, and soon became a wealthy investor, promoter and entrepreneur in a variety of enterprises.

During the depression of the seventies, with all kinds of businesses going bankrupt all around him, he took a daring step and concentrated all his resources and energies in the making of steel. He hired the best people in steel technology and plant management, and eventually defeated all his rivals in the field.

When he sold this business to the United States Steel Corporation in 1901 he found himself to be one of the richest men in the world, with $250 million in US Steel bonds.

Making use of wealth

Carnegie never forgot that wealth should be used to help other people.

A moral duty

Carnegie proclaimed that it was the moral duty of all possessors of great wealth to plough back their money into philanthropy with the same judgment, zeal and leadership they had devoted to getting rich.

Practise what you preach

Carnegie lived up to that precept: paying for thousands of library buildings, setting up trusts, founding foundations, endowing universities, and creating trust funds.

Carnegie Hall

Most famous of all his works were Carnegie Hall in New York and the Peace Palace at The Hague.

Dying rich

The man who dies rich dies disgraced.

A daring risk-taking

If Carnegie had not been a daring risk-taker, nobody would have heard of him.

Money can't buy everything

Millionaires seldom smile.

Plumbing and philosophy

The society which scorns excellence in plumbing because plumbing is a humble activity, and tolerates shoddiness in philosophy because philosophy is an exalted activity, will have neither good plumbing nor good philosophy. Neither its pipes nor its theories will hold water.

John W. Gardner, President of the Carnegie Foundation

Dreaming

Refuse to accept anything

It's a funny thing about life – if you refuse to accept anything but the best you very often get it.
Somerset Maugham

Follow your dream

If one advances confidently in the direction of his dreams, and endeavours to live the life which he has imagined, he will meet with a success unexpected in common hours.
Henry David Thoreau

The need for depth

To reach a great height a person needs to have great depth.
Author unknown

Making your dreams come true

No dream comes true until you wake up and go to work.
Author unknown

The dream

The dream is not about getting rich but about making a difference.
Bill Gates

Originality versus imitation

It is better to fail in originality than to succeed in imitation.
Herman Melville

Believing in dreams

The future belongs to those who believe in the beauty of their dreams.
Eleanor Roosevelt

The dream of the United Nations

What has happened to the dream of the United Nations' founders? What has happened to the spirit which created the United Nations? The answer is clear: governments got in the way of the dreams of the people.
>   Ronald Reagan, to the General Assembly of the United Nations, 1983

The impossible dream

Dream the impossible dream. Dreaming it may make it possible. It often has.
>   Author unknown

Follow your dreams

Go confidently in the direction of your dreams! Live the life you've imagined.
>   Henry David Thoreau

Realize your dreams

Don't be a reader only, do something, realize your dreams.
>   Author unknown

Vision without action

Vision without action is a daydream.
Action without vision is a nightmare.
>   Japanese proverb

Positive attitudes towards oneself

Make the most of yourself

Make the most of yourself, for that is all there is of you.
   Ralph Waldo Emerson

Still waters

A life all turbulence and noise may seem
To him that leads it wise and to be praised,
But wisdom is a pearl with most success
Sought in still waters.
   William Cowper, *The Task*, volume 3

Questions to ask yourself each day

1. How can I do better?
2. How can I do more?
3. How can I be a better listener?

Am I positive about the little I do do?

Don't be afraid to give your best to what seemingly are small jobs. Every time you conquer one it makes you that much stronger. If you do the little jobs well, the big ones will tend to take care of themselves.
   Dale Carnegie

Do I pat myself on the back for being busy?

It is not enough to be busy. The question is: what are we busy about?
   Henry David Thoreau

Concluding thought

I ceased to be lord over myself. I was no longer the captain of my soul, and did not know it. I allowed pleasure to dominate me.
   Oscar Wilde

Helen Keller

The life of Helen Keller is an amazing example of the triumph of the human spirit over physical disability. Next time you feel down, think of Helen Keller.

She was born physically normal in Tuscumbia, Alabama, but lost her sight and hearing as a toddler. On the advice of Alexander Graham Bell, her parents applied to the Perkins Institute for the Blind in Boston for a teacher, and hired Anne Mansfield Sullivan. Through Sullivan's extraordinary instruction, Helen, as a little girl, learned to communicate with the world around her. From Sullivan, Helen learned to read and write in Braille. She went on to be an influential organizer, and fundraiser for handicapped people.

She became a great inspiration to many through her writings, even though she remained blind, deaf and dumb.

Sayings of Helen Keller
Life is ...

Life is either a daring adventure or nothing at all. Life is an exciting business, and it is most exciting when it is lived for others.

Character is ...

Character cannot be developed in ease and quiet. Only through experiences of trial and suffering can the soul be strengthened, vision cleared, ambition inspired and success achieved.

The heart

The best and most beautiful things in the world cannot be seen, not touched ... but are felt in the heart.

Apathy

Science may have found a cure for most evils, but it has found no remedy for the worst of them all – the apathy of human beings.

Adversity

We could never learn to be brave and patient if there were only joy in the world.

Positive attitudes towards learning

Learning as a life-time occupation

We live in a time of such rapid change and growth of knowledge that only he who is in a fundamental sense a scholar – that is, a person who continues to learn and inquire – can hope to keep pace, let alone play the role of guide.

Nathan M. Pusey, President of Harvard

Keep on learning

As long as you live, keep learning how to live.

Seneca

No more inventions are possible!

Everything that can be invented has been invented.

Charles Duell, Director of the US Patent Office, 1899

Flying is impossible

Heavier-than-air flying machines are impossible.

President of the British Royal Society, 1895

Computers have no market

I think there is a world market for maybe five computers.

Thomas Watson, Chairman of IBM, 1943

If you think ...

If you think you are beaten, you are;
If you think you dare not, you don't.
If you like to win, but you think you can't,
It is almost certain you won't.

If you think you'll lose, you've lost,
For out of the world you'll find
Increase begins with a fellow's believing –
It's all in his state of mind.

If you think you are outclassed, you are;
You've got to think higher to rise.
You've got to believe in yourself before
You can ever win the prize.

Life's battles don't always go
To the stronger or faster man;
But sooner or later, the man who wins
is the man *who thinks he can!*
Author unknown

Don't be put off by what you can't achieve

Do not let what you cannot do interfere with what you can do.
John Wooden, considered the greatest coach in the history of US college basketball

Attitude is everything

Any fact facing us is not as important as our attitude towards it. Our attitude determines our success or failure.

Admit your own ignorance

You do ill if you praise, but worse if you censure what you do not understand.
Leonardo da Vinci

To be great

To be great, concentrate. Most people remain ordinary because they scatter their energies.
Author unknown

Self-belief

Beliefs and interests

One person with a belief is equal to a force of 99 who have only interests.
John Stuart Mill

Belief and conquering

For they can conquer who believe they can.
Virgil

Self-pity

Self-pity in its early stages is as snug as a feather mattress. Only when it hardens does it become uncomfortable.
Maya Angelou

Self-pity is easily the most destructive of the non-pharmaceutical narcotics; it is addictive, gives momentary pleasure and separates the victim from reality.
John W. Gardner, President of the Carnegie Foundation

Putting yourself down

No one can make you feel inferior without your consent.
Eleanor Roosevelt

So says the president

Risking all

No man is worth his salt who is not ready at all times to risk his body, to risk his well-being, to risk his life in a great cause.
Theodore Roosevelt

Body language

Concentrate on what the eyes are saying

When the eyes say one thing and the tongue another, the practised person relies on the language of the first.
   Ralph Waldo Emerson

Thank you, Charles Darwin

We have Charles Darwin to thank for alerting us to the significance of facial expressions and body language. His book, *The Expression of the Emotions in Man and Animals*, although published way back in 1872, still greatly influences this subject today. However, it is only since the 1960s that the study of non-verbal communication has really taken off.

Looking into people

You must look into people, as well as at them.
   Lord Chesterfield

Looking at children and pets

It's easy to see that a six-year-old jumping up and down, smiling broadly, and clapping his hands together is 'jumping for joy'.

When a cat, and some dogs, are totally happy and relaxed they roll over so that their tummies are exposed for us to tickle.

Generally speaking, openness is a sign of well-being, while being all closed up in our sitting or standing postures is one of nervousness or defensiveness.

Type of communication	Percentage
Verbal/words (including tone of voice)	35–40
Non-verbal	60–65

Verbal communication is often split up into 'verbal' and 'vocal' communication. 'Verbal' means words. These are the actual words used in the communication and account for less than 10% of our communication, as about 30% of our spoken communication is in the form of inflection and tone of voice, which is often called 'vocal' communication. Clearly, non-verbal communication is important. It has been estimated that most people speak for less than 15 minutes per day.

What is there to learn from non-verbal communication?

1. What people are thinking, when they are not speaking.
2. What a person's attitude towards you is.
3. In a meeting, how different people are reacting to different ideas and to each other.

Where can I learn about non-verbal communication?

1. From the TV. Switch down the sound and just observe the body language you see.
2. Watch a silent movie, starring Laurel and Hardy or Charlie Chaplin.
3. Go to an airport and observe people waiting to greet, and greeting, passengers.

Type of non-verbal communication	Probable meaning

1. Handshake
   a. Two handed
   b. Holding the wrist
   c. Holding the elbow
   d. Holding the upper arm
   e. Holding the shoulder
	You can trust me. Often used by politicians. When a person uses their left hand during a handshake he is communicating more than a mere handshake with the right hand only. The degree of warmth increases from the hand, to the elbow to the upper arm to the shoulder.

2. The shoulder shrug	I've no idea what you're talking about.
3. Palms a. Palm uppermost	I'm being honest and open and I'm making a non-threatening request.
b. Palm facing down	I'm in charge here.
c. Closed palm, pointing finger	Do as I say, or else.

4. Legs
   a. Sitting crossed leg — I'm not too happy to be here.
   b. Sitting crossed leg and folded arms — I'm fed up with being here.
   c. Standing crossed legs, folded arms — This is my defence posture.
   d. Standing legs not crossed, palms facing up — Do you like me? I'm being open to you.

5. Hands
   a. Clenched hands, hands on table — A show of hostility.
   b. Clenched hands, in raised position — Even more hostile than hands on table.
   c. Hands forming a raised steeple shape — I'm in charge here.
   d. Hands clasped together — Anxiety or I'm in charge.

6. Thumbs
   a. Thumbs up gesture — Everything is OK.
   b. Hand holding lapel with thumb uppermost. — I am superior to you lot.
   c. Thumb protruding from pocket — I am the dominant type.

7. Hands linked to mouth gestures
   a. Hand, or some fingers, over mouth — I've just told a lie.
   b. Finger rubbing bottom of nose — I've just told a lie.
   c. Pulling the collar — I've just told a lie.
   d. Scratching the neck, just below the ear — I don't agree with you.
   e. Fingers in mouth — I'm in need of some reassurance.
   f. A mouth block: touching mouth with a pair of glasses — I'm resisting what you say.
   g. The 'L' chin rest: leaning chin on thumb, index finger on side of face — I'm making a critical evaluation.

Body language

8. Arms
   a. Normal folded arms — I'm taking up a defensive position.
   b. Folded arms with fists clenched — I'm on the war-path.
   c. Folded arms, hands gripping under arms — I'm scared, but am not going to show it.
   d. Folded arms, with thumbs stuck up — I'm the top dog and very superior to you.
   e. Holding one's own hand in front of one — I'm fearful and need of some reassurance.

9. Feet
   a. When standing, feet crossed — This is my defensive pose.
   b. When standing, feet uncrossed — This is my open pose.
   c. Feet pointing in someone's direction — I like that person.

10. Other forms of non-verbal communication
    a. Holding a posy of flowers in front — I'm using these flowers as a barrier.
    b. Picking of a pretend piece of dust from one's sleeve. — I disapprove of what you said.
    c. Hands behind head, seated, ankle crossed on knee — One day you'll be smart like me.
    d. Hands on hips — Do I appeal to you?
    e. Seated, hands on knees, leaning forward — Let's finish this meeting *now*.
    f. Leaning back in chair, hands behind head — I'm confident, I'm superior.
    g. Leaning on table — I'm involved. I'm in authority here.
    h. Leaning against a wall, on one leg, other leg crossed. — I'm in my casual mode.

Change yourself

Being

The way to live is to be.
    Lao Tzu, *Tao Te Ching*

Make a success of your life

There is a time to succeed in life and a time to make a success of your life.
    Brigitte Bardot's favourite saying of La Rochefoucauld

Ennoble your works

One must not always think so much about what one should do, but what one should be.
Our works do not ennoble us; but we must ennoble our works.
    Meister Eckhart

Wisdom and enlightenment

Knowing others is wisdom. Knowing the self is enlightenment.
    Lao Tzu, *Tao Te Ching*

Peace of mind

With peace of mind a poor man is rich; without it, a rich man is poor.
    Author unknown

Keep yourself in peace

First keep yourself in peace, and then you will be able to pacify others.
  A peaceable man does more than a learned one.
    Thomas à Kempis

A changed person can overcome obstacles

Obstacles are those frightful things you see when you take your eyes off your goal.
    Henry Ford

Perseverance

By way of introduction ...

Nothing can take the place of persistence.
Talent will not:
   Thousands with talents are drifters.
Genius will not:
   Unrewarded genius is almost a proverb.
Education will not:
   The world is full of educated derelicts.
Persistence alone solves all the world's big problems.
   Author unknown

So says the president

Persistence and determination

Nothing in the world can take the place of perseverance. Talent will not; nothing is more common than unsuccessful men with talent. Genius will not; unrewarded genius is almost a proverb. Persistence and determination alone are omnipotent.
   Calvin Coolidge

1800 driving lessons

In February 1997 Sue Evans-Jones, from Yate, near Bristol, England, passed her driving test. She had had ten driving instructors over a period of 27 years, and had spent over £20,000 on her 1800 driving lessons.

Longitude

Dava Sobel was turned down by ten British publishers before her first novel, Longitude, was published. The story about John Harrison's struggle to invent a chronometer made Sobel into a millionairess in 23 weeks, as her book topped the best-selling lists for half a year.

About average

If at first you don't succeed – you are about average.

Perseverance is ...

Perseverance is
>the sister of patience,
>the daughter of constancy,
>the friend of peace,
>the cementer of friendships,
>the bond of harmony
>and the bulwark of holiness.
>Bernard of Clairvaux, *The Song of Songs*

Abraham Lincoln

Lincoln (1809–1865), born in the backwoods of Kentucky, worked as a rail splitter, boatman, postmaster, surveyor, storekeeper, lawyer, state legislator and congressman before gaining national attention during debates for election to the US Senate. When he was elected the 16th US President, seven states had already seceded from the Union, to be followed by four more. He guided the US through five years of traumatic civil war and issued the Emancipation Proclamation to outlaw slavery in the USA. His Gettysburg Address, written on the train ride to the battlefield, is still considered a masterpiece.

Perseverance in politics

- Abraham Lincoln failed in business in 1831.
- Was defeated for legislature in 1832.
- Had a second business failure in 1833.
- Suffered a nervous breakdown in 1836.
- Was defeated as candidate for Speaker in 1838.
- Was defeated as candidate for Elector in 1840.
- Was defeated as candidate for Congress in 1848.
- Was defeated as candidate for Senate in 1858.
- Was elected President in 1860.

Finish the work

> With malice toward none;
> with charity for all;
> with firmness in the right,
> as God gives us to see the right –
> let us strive on to finish the work we are in.
> **Abraham Lincoln**

A battle against polio

You are looking at a man who spent two years trying to learn to wiggle his big toe.

> Franklin D. Roosevelt, when asked how he could do so much without becoming tired, referring to his long fight against polio

A saying to ponder

> 'Tis a lesson you should heed,
> Try, try again.
> If at first you don't succeed.
> Try, try again.
> **William Edward Dickson, 'Try and Try Again'**

The last lap

I have seen too many men fall out in the last lap.

> Author unknown; a man explaining why he would not consent to any writing his biography during his lifetime

Concluding thought

There are only two creatures that can surmount the pyramids: the eagle and the snail.

> **Eastern proverb**

Prepare and act

So says the president

I will study
I will study and get ready, and maybe my chance will come.

Chopping down a tree
If I had eight hours to chop down a tree, I'd spend six sharpening my axe.
   Abraham Lincoln

Do it now!
Do it now! Today will be yesterday tomorrow.

Cuba's revolution
I began revolution with 82 men. If I had [to] do it again, I would do it with 10 or 15 and absolute faith. It does not matter how small you are if you have faith and plan of action.
   Fidel Castro

Do all the good you can
   Do all the good you can,
   in all the ways you can,
   to all the souls you can,
   in every place you can,
   at all the times you can,
   with all the zeal you can,
   as long as ever you can.
   John Wesley

All I did …
All I was doing was trying to get home from work.
   Rosa Parks, recalling her refusal to move to the back of a bus, which sparked the civil rights movement in 1965, in Birmingham, Alabama, USA

Making decisions

Standing on one leg

He who deliberates fully before taking a step will spend his entire life on one leg.
Chinese proverb

Doing nothing

In any moment of decision the best thing you can do is the right thing, the next best thing is the wrong thing, and the worst thing you can do is nothing.
Theodore Roosevelt

Taking decisions

A decision is the action an executive must take when he has information so incomplete that the answer does not suggest itself.
Admiral Arthur W. Redford, Former Chairman, Joint Chiefs of Staff (US Navy)

Perspective

There is more to life than 'me' and 'now'. The bigger picture produces better quality decisions.

The value of time

Know the true value of time; snatch, seize and enjoy every moment of it. No idleness; no laziness; no procrastination: never put off till tomorrow what you can do today.
Lord Chesterfield

Twin brothers

Indecision and procrastination are twin brothers. Where one is found, the other may usually be found also.

part three

Overcoming Problems

So you failed!

Do you remember Robert the Bruce and the spider?

King Robert the Bruce of Scotland, hounded after being defeated in battle, took refuge in a lonely cave, where he began to make plans. Everything looked so grim for him that he was tempted to despair. He almost lost heart and gave up, when he spotted something moving close to his head. This spider was carefully and painfully attempting to climb up a slender thread to its web in a concealed corner of the cave.

The king watched as it made several unsuccessful attempts to get to the top. As the spider kept on falling to the ground, again and again, Robert the Bruce thought how its efforts typified his own unsuccessful efforts to win victories to rid Scotland of her enemies. Like the spider, he never seemed to reach the place he was aiming at. But the despondent king kept watching the spider's movements.

> Steadily, steadily, inch by inch,
> Higher and higher he got,
> Till a neat little run, at the very last pinch
> Put him into his native cot.

Robert the Bruce took courage from this persevering spider and left the cave an inspired man

A fact to ponder

Agatha Christie had her first novel turned down by seventeen publishers.

Failure: what it does mean, what it doesn't mean

Failure doesn't mean you are a failure;
　it *does* mean you haven't yet succeeded.
Failure doesn't mean you have accomplished nothing;
　it *does* mean you have learned something.

Failure doesn't mean that you have been a fool;
   it *does* mean you have a lot of faith.
Failure doesn't mean you have been disgraced;
   it *does* mean you were willing to try.
Failure doesn't mean you don't have it;
   it *does* mean you have to do something in a different way.
Failure doesn't mean you are inferior;
   it *does* mean you are not perfect.
Failure doesn't mean you wasted your life;
   it *does* mean you have a reason to start afresh.
Failure doesn't mean you should give up;
   it *does* mean you must try harder.
Failure doesn't mean you will never make it;
   it *does* mean it will take a little longer.
Failure doesn't mean God has abandoned you;
   it *does* mean God has a better way.
   Author unknown

Concluding thought

Our greatest glory is not in never failing, but in rising every time we fall.
   Confucius

The stress rating scale

Many of today's stress rating scales stem from the work of Dr Thomas Holmes and Dr Richard Rahe, of the University of Washington in Seattle, USA. Back in the 1960s they published in chart form, in the Journal of Psychosomatic Research, what they called 'the degrees of stress'.

From their research, on this stress rating scale they plotted, from 1–100, how different events in our lives affect us.

How to read the scale

- Not everyone is affected by stress in the same way.
- Stress is seen to be commonly associated with life events.
- It provides a comprehensive checklist of the causes of stress which affect us all.

For example, losing a job may bring more stress than marriage to some people, even though the stress rating scale puts it the other way round.

The top of the scale

The death of a wife or husband was put at the top of the scale, with a rating of 100. The numbers stand for the amount of stress each event is likely to cause.

The top three were all linked to marriage. In order they were:
- Death of a spouse
- Divorce

> A divorce is like an amputation: you survive, but there's less of you.
>
> Margaret Atwood

- Marital separation

Going down the scale

Following a jail sentence, comes a death in the family.

> It is a gaping wound, whenever one touches it and removes the bandages and plasters of daily life.
>
> Winston Churchill, letter to his wife, Clementine, after the death of their daughter, Marigold

Then, rated in the 50s and 40s are
- Personal injury/illness
- Marriage
- Losing a job
- Marital reconciliation
- Retirement

> They look upon retirement as something between euthanasia and castration.
>
> **Leon A. Danco, President of the Centre for Family Business, on company founders who liken 'giving up' to planning their own funerals**

- Serious illness of family member

> Knowing what I now know, I still would have ordered the defoliation to achieve the objectives it did, of reducing casualties. That does not ease the sorrow I feel for Elmo, or the anguish his illness, and Russell's disability, give me. It is the first thing I think of when I awake in the morning, and the last thing I remember when I go to sleep at night.
>
> **Admiral Elmo Zumwalt Junior, former US Chief of Naval Operations, speaking of his son suffering from cancer and his grandson from a debilitating learning disorder**

- Pregnancy

The stress rating of 39

The stress rating of 39 proved to be a popular one. Three events all tied with this rating:
- Sex problems
- New baby
- Business readjustment

Finance and problems at home

Financial problems and difficulties at home loomed large in the 30s and 20s of the stress scale. Going down the list we find: change in financial situation; death of a close friend; change of job; increased arguments with wife/husband; large mortgage or loan.

Tied on 29 were three events:
- New work load
- Children leaving home
- Trouble with in-laws

Then came:
- Outstanding personal achievement
- Husband or wife begins or stops work
- Moving home
- Changes at work, home, college or school
- Change in social activities
- Change in sleeping habits
- Change in eating habits

Christmas and stress

Some of the events on the scale may be a little surprising. For example, not everyone would have thought of putting Christmas on their 'stress scale'.

After 'holiday' and before a 'minor violation of the law' came 'Christmas' with a stress rating of 12.

Using the scale

You hardly need to be a top psychologist to realize that a person who is going through a divorce, and so moves home, and maybe 'loses' children, will be under great stress at work. However, the scale does point out, in a general way, what events cause serious stress on most of us.

Stress management

Underload

Insufficient stimulus and challenge is one of the biggest causes of dissatisfaction at work.

Stress and motivation

The right kind of motivation reduces stress.

The source of stress

Contrary to what is often believed, stress does not actually derive directly from external causes, but is to a large extent self-generated. Situations are not in themselves stressful – it is our reactions which make them so.

How to cope with pressure

a. Raise your own awareness about pressure
   It's hard to manage without understanding; we can't deal with something unless we know it's there.
b. Accept responsibility
   People blame their circumstances for avoiding action. We will never manage pressure as long as we think that it's someone else's responsibility to do it for us.
c. Take action
   The universe rewards action, not thought. There are millions of people who think up wonderful ways for making money. Only the ones who do something about it get rich.
d. Monitor progress
   Unless we monitor consciously our ability to manage pressure, we run the risk of slipping into a pattern of behaviour that produces stress instead of high performance.

Pressure is cumulative

A person, like a pressure cooker, has a limited capacity. Take note of the main life events which cause pressure, such as moving house, the death of a partner, close friend or relative.

Boredom and burn-out

Boredom and burn-out both kill. Too little pressure or too much pressure can both be harmful.

Burn-out

At one end of the scale we have a pressure overload. People can no longer cope and may suffer from a major mental or physical breakdown. This is known as 'burn-out'.

Boredom

At the other extreme, people have so little stimulation they become lethargic and lose their ability to cope with everyday life. This lack of pressure or stimulation over long periods of time is called 'rust out'. This stems from John Wesley's quip that he would prefer to wear out rather than rust out.

Keys to stress management

1. Appreciate the potential value of stress in creating incentive, which we all need.
2. Get to know yourself and become fully aware of your personality type. Remember that stress is caused from within and is best dealt with from within. So become aware of your own stress levels.
3. Identify sources of stress inherent in your own lifestyle.
4. Avoid perfectionism, expecting too much of self and others.
5. Avoid unnecessarily provoking situations where this is possible.
6. Avoid over-committing yourself. Learn when to say 'no' without feeling guilty.
7. Know how to avoid causing stress to others.
8. Learn the value of positive thinking. Discover how effective a positive outlook can be.
9. Acquire the habit of sorting out your priorities.

Stress-induced ailments

- high blood pressure
- heart disease

- ulcers
- headaches
- insomnia
- panic attacks
- depression
- anxiety
- loss of concentration
- angry outbursts
- phobias

Try to be the first to recognize these symptoms in yourself and in others.

DIY stress audit: assessing the causes of stress

1. How satisfied are you with ...
- your physical working conditions?
- your wage packet?
- your job security?

Give the questions a rating on a scale of 1–10.
1= unbelievably bad; 10 = absolutely wonderful.

2. During the past month, how much of the time has the job made you feel ...
- fulfilled?
- irritable?
- tense?
- calm?

Give the questions a rating on a scale of 1–10.
1 = Every day; 10 = never.

Smiling

The first 'Laughter Clinic' in Great Britain was opened in 1992 by the National Health Service in Birmingham. Patients who suffer from stress go there and are taught to use laughter to relax.

Smile

When people are happy they smile, but when they are sad, they look depressed.
    Proverbs 15:13

Spread a smile

Most smiles are started by other smiles. Smile first.
    Author unknown

The MotivAider

The cost of stress

We may not be impressed to learn the exact cost of stress on a nation's economy. It has been estimated that it costs the American economy $100 billion a year. We are, however, very concerned about the toll stress takes on us individually. Stress 'costs' us so much:

- It puts relationships under strain.
- It robs us of our productivity.
- It threatens our health.

Enter the MotivAider

Most stress reducing methods are ineffective because they are never carried out by us. The *MotivAider* sets out to change all this. How? By giving us 'follow through'.

For example, if you need to mentally clean the slate of accumulated stress, you could periodically take a deep abdominal breath. It's as easy as that.

But you don't do it, because you don't remember to do it. The problem is, no matter how motivated you are, you keep forgetting to take a simple stress reducing action.

The MotivAider is …

The *MotivAider* is a powerful tool, according to its own advert, that gives you the power to follow through. The *MotivAider* is a simple electronic device invented by a clinical psychologist to solve the complex problem of poor follow through.

A gentle, noiseless vibration

Through a gentle, noiseless vibration, the *MotivAider* periodically reminds you to carry out the actions you have chosen to reduce stress.

When the *MotivAider* is activated, no one else knows because it is completely silent and it is small enough to fit on a belt or in a pocket.

How it works

You have decided to reduce stress at work by remaining focused on the task in hand. At the start of the day you are determined to ignore all the other projects screaming for your attention. But, by the end of the day, you are reduced to being a nervous wreck. You still end up worrying about all the work that you still have to do.

To use the MotivAider

1. Make up a personal message. For example, it could be *'one thing at a time'*.
2. Attach your message to the *MotivAider*. So, when the *MotivAider* vibrates, you will remember *'one thing at a time'*.
3. Set your *MotivAider* so that it reminds you of your message as often as you desire. This could be once a day, once an hour or every ten minutes.
4. Turn the power switch on and slip the *MotivAider* into your pocket, on to your belt or waistband. Now you're *MotivAided*!

Motivation

If you must have motivation, think of your pay cheque on Friday.
   Noël Coward, advice to actors

Greed

Craving for money

The most grievous kind of destitution is to want money in the midst of wealth.
    Seneca

Craving

Craving, not having, is the mother of a reckless giving of oneself.
    Eric Hoffer

Business and money

A business that makes nothing but money is a poor kind of business.
    Henry Ford

Contentment

He who doesn't find a little enough, will find nothing enough.
    Epicurus

Loving money

My father loves names and Jackie loves money.
    Alexander Onassis, when his father Aristotle Onassis married Jacqueline Kennedy

Counting money

If you can count your money you don't have a billion dollars.
    J. Paul Getty

Painting money

I asked around 10 or 15 people for suggestions ... Finally one lady friend asked the right question, 'Well, what do you love most?' That's how I started painting money.
    Andy Warhol

Liking money

Liking money like I like it, is nothing less than mysticism. Money is a glory.

Salvador Dali

> ### Aesop's fables
>
> A dog was crossing a river with a piece of meat in her mouth. As she spotted her own reflection in the water she thought that she saw another dog with a larger piece of meat in its mouth. She let go of her own piece of meat and attempted to snatch the other piece of meat from the other dog. This resulted in her having neither piece of meat. She could not grab the other piece of meat, as it did not exist, and the river carried her own piece of meat down stream.
>
> Moral: This story illustrates what happens to people who always want more than they have.

Greed and the environment

If we go on the way we have, the fault is our greed [and] if we are not willing [to change], we will disappear from the face of the globe, to be replaced by the insect.

Jacques Cousteau

Craving wealth

Whoever craves wealth is like a man who drinks sea water; the more he drinks, the more he increases his thirst, and he does not cease to drink until he perishes.

According to a Muslim tradition, this was said by Jesus Christ

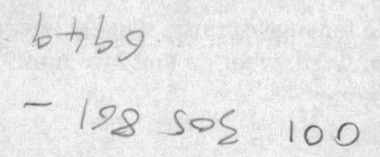

Fearing fear

A darkroom

Fear is a darkroom for developing negatives.
   Anonymous

Fearing old age

I'm not interested in age. People who tell me their age are silly. You're as old as you feel.
   Elizabeth Arden

Fearing fear

The only thing we have to fear is fear itself.
   Franklin D. Roosevelt

The only thing I am afraid of is fear.
   Duke of Wellington

He has not learnt a lesson of life, who does not every day surmount a fear. Do the thing you fear, and the death of fear is certain.
   Ralph Waldo Emerson

There is perhaps nothing so bad and so dangerous in life as fear.
   Jawaharlal Nehru

Face the storms

Try riding a bicycle up a hill at night – it's easier than during the day, when you can see the whole hill looming up in front of you!

The mastery of fear

Courage is resistance to fear, mastery of fear, not absence of fear.
   Mark Twain

Suffering fear

A man who fears suffering is already suffering from what he fears.
Michel de Montaigne

God's sunshine

Never once since the world began
   Has the sun ever stopped shining.
His face very often we could not see,
And we grumbled at his inconstancy;
But the clouds were really to blame, not he,
   For, behind them, he was shining.

And so – behind life's darkest clouds
   God's love is always shining.
We veil it at times with our faithless fears,
And darken our sight with our foolish tears,
But in time the atmosphere always clears,
   For his love is always shining.
John Oxenham

> ### So says the president
> Let us never negotiate out of fear. Let us never fear to negotiate.
> John F. Kennedy

Beating your fear

Isolate your fear

Do you know what you fear?

Write it down. Make a list of your fears, no matter how long the list turns out to be. Then figure out an action plan to defeat your fear.

Don't be ashamed of seeking help to do this – help may be in the form of a close friend or a doctor.

The wise take action

The wise see knowledge and action as one; they see truly.
    Bhagavad Gita

Action cures fear. Inaction strengthens fear.

Type of fear	Action plan to beat it
1. Fear of people	Remember: other people are only people – just like you.

2. Fear of what people say	Is your plan of action right? If so go ahead. People who are never criticized for anything are those who do nothing.
	'To escape criticism
	  do nothing,
	    say nothing,
	      be nothing.'
	        Elbert Hubbard
	
	'If you fear making anyone mad,
	  then you ultimately probe
	    for the lowest common
	    denominator
	      of human achievement.'
	        Jimmy Carter

3. Fear of failing exams — Join the club! Everyone fears this, so try not to worry. Just study. You can only do the best in the time you have left.

4. Fear about things I can't control — This is quite irrational, and tell yourself that this is the case.

Act in a confident way

If you act in a confident way it helps you to become a confident person.
1. Look people in the eye. Don't be for ever looking down at the ground.
2. Smile. Don't go around with a constant scowl on your face.

Pride and prejudice

Aesop's fables

Pride goes before a fall

The mice and the weasels were at war, and the mice were always coming off worse. The mice held a meeting in which they concluded that their defeats were due to lack of leadership. So they appointed from their ranks some mice to be generals. These generals, to make sure that they could be distinguished from the rest of the mice, made horns and attached them to their heads.

In the next battle between the mice and the weasels the whole mice army was routed and had to flee. All the mice reached their holes safely, except for the generals, who, unable to get into their holes because of their horns, were seized and eaten.

Moral: Vainglory is often the cause of misfortune.

The victor is defeated

A cock that had come off worst in a fight with his rival for the affections of the hens went and hid himself in a dark corner. Meanwhile, the victor climbed on to a high wall where he crowed at the top of his voice. Without any warning, an eagle swooped down and snatched it up. The other cock was kept safe in his hiding place and was now able to continue wooing the hens without any fear of being interrupted.

Moral: This story shows how God resists the proud but gives grace to the humble.

Prejudice

A student once went up to a well-known evangelist and said, 'I've made up my mind, don't confuse me with facts!'

The wise evangelist replied, 'There is nothing so deadly as a closed mind, ' and then proceeded to tell this story. 'There was a man who once thought that he was dead. Nothing that his parents, doctors, friends or psychiatrists could do could persuade him otherwise. One psychiatrist, however, worked out a plan of action. After studying together a medical textbook he managed to convince the man of one simple fact: dead men do not bleed.

'"Yes, I agree," said the man, "dead men do not bleed," whereupon the psychiatrist plunged a small knife into the man's arm and the blood started to flow. The man looked at his arm, his face white with astonishment and horror. "Goodness me," he said, "dead men bleed after all!"'

The history of prejudice

First woman MP

Nancy Witcher Langhorne Astor (1879–1964) became the first woman to sit as a Member of Parliament in the British House of Commons, when she took her seat in 1919. She supported the women's rights and temperance movements.

The suffragettes

Emily Wilding Davison (1872–1913), an English suffragette, tried to grab the reins of the racehorse owned by the king near the end of the 1913 Derby race. She died from her injuries a few days later.

Britain's first woman doctor

Elizabeth Garrett Anderson (1836–1917) was the first woman doctor allowed to practise in England. Against great prejudice from male doctors, she passed her medical examinations in 1865 and worked in the East London hospital. In 1874 she founded the London School of Medicine for Women and became the first woman mayor in England, when she was elected Mayor of Aldeburgh, in Suffolk, her birthplace.

Women in society

Why have women passion, intellect, moral activity – these three – and a place in society where not one of these three can be exercised?
   Florence Nightingale

Making mistakes

Mistakes are part of life
Mistakes are part of the dues one pays for a full life.
   Sophia Loren

Don't be afraid of errors
Be bold. If you're going to make an error, make a doozey, and don't be afraid to hit the ball.
   Billie Jean King

If you've never made a mistake ...
The man who makes no mistakes does not usually make anything.
   Edward John Phelps

Everyone makes mistakes
There is no one on earth who does what is right and never makes a mistake.
   Ecclesiastes 7:20

Creative mistakes
Anyone who has never made a mistake has never tried anything new.
   Albert Einstein

So says the president
Achieving
Only those who dare to fail greatly can ever achieve greatly.
   Robert F. Kennedy

Anger

What makes you angry?
A man is as big as the things that make him angry.
    Winston Churchill

Arguments, answering back
Never answer an angry word with an angry word.
It's always the second remark that starts the trouble.
    Author unknown

A gentle answer
A gentle answer quietens anger.
    Proverbs 15:1

Ten wise sayings about anger

1. He who angers you, conquers you.
   Proverb

2. Anger is only one letter, and one second, away from danger.
   Author unknown

3. Anger is short madness.
   Horace, *Epistles*

4. Never forget what a person says to you when he is angry.
   Henry Ward Beecher

5. Anger blows out the lamp of the mind.
   Author unknown

6. No matter how just your words may be, you ruin everything when you speak with anger.
   John Chrysosdom

7. Anger is a child's reaction to an adult situation.
   Author unknown

8. To seek to extinguish anger utterly is but a bravery of the Stoics. We have better oracles: 'Be angry, but sin not'; 'Let not the sun go down upon your wrath.'
   Francis Bacon

9. He that is slow to anger is better than the mighty; and he that ruleth his spirit than he that taketh a city.
   Proverbs 16:32 (AV).

10. Anger is short-lived in a good man.
    Thomas Fuller, *Gnomologia*

To be positively angry

A man that does not know how to be angry does not know how to be good. And man that does not know how to be shaken to his heart's core with indignation over things evil is either a fungus or a wicked man.
   Henry Ward Beecher

Anger is one of the sinews of the soul. He who lacks it hath a maimed mind.
   Thomas Fuller, *Gnomologia*

Anybody can become angry – that is easy;
but to be angry with the right person, and to the right degree,
and at the right time, and for the right purpose,
and in the right way – that is not within everybody's power and it is not easy.
   Aristotle

Soft and hard

Use soft words and hard arguments.
   English proverb

Speaking with the irrational

It is useless for us to reason a man out of a thing he has never been reasoned into.
   Jonathan Swift

Life beyond anger

Once I got past my anger toward my mother, I began to excel in volleyball and modelling.
   Super-model Gabrielle Reece

A negative reaction

Never react to abuse by passing it on.

Staying angry

Anger only dwells in the bosom of fools.
   Albert Einstein

Concluding thought

The start of an argument is like the first break in a dam; stop it before it goes any further.
   Proverbs 17:14

Worry

'Worry': derived from the Anglo-Saxon word meaning 'to strangle' or 'to choke'.

Anxiety

Anxiety does not empty tomorrow of its sorrows, but only empties today of its strength.
   C.H. Spurgeon

Smiling versus frowning

It takes 45 muscles of the face to frown but only 17 to smile.
   Author unknown

The worried cow

> The worried cow would have lived till now
>   If she had saved her breath;
> But she feared her hay wouldn't last all day,
>   And she mooed herself to death.

Taylor Smith

Worry and hurry

'Don't you worry and don't you hurry.' I know that phrase by heart, and if all the other music perish out of the world it would still sing to me.
   Mark Twain

Fret

A hundred years' fret will not pay a penny of debt.
   French proverb

Anxiety is a great evil

Anxiety is the greatest evil that can befall us except sin; for just as revolt and sedition in a country cause havoc and sap its resistance to a foreign invasion, so we, when troubled and worried, are unable to preserve the virtues we have already acquired, or resist

the temptations of the devil, who then diligently fishes, as they say, in troubled waters.
Francis de Sales

Learning from the birds

Good morning, theologians! You wake and sing. But I, old fool, know less than you and worry over everything, instead of simply trusting in the heavenly Father's care.
Martin Luther, talking to the birds as he walked through the woods

Tomorrow has two handles

Tomorrow has two handles: the handle of fear and the handle of faith. You can take hold of it by either handle.
Author unknown

Augustine's advice

In all trouble you should seek God. You should not set him over against your troubles, but within them. God can only relieve your troubles if you in your anxiety cling to him. Trouble should not really be thought of as this thing or that in particular, for our whole life on earth involves trouble; and through the troubles of our earthly pilgrimage we find God.
Augustine, *Discourses on the Psalms*

Nothing is worth worrying about

Nothing in the affairs of men is worthy of great anxiety.
Plato, *The Republic*

The modern plague

Anxiety is the great modern plague.
Dr Smiled Blanton

Criticism

Aesop's fables

Criticism of others

Once upon a time when Prometheus made people, he hung two bags around their necks. One bag hung down in front of them, and was full of other people's defects, and one bag hung down behind them, and was full of their own faults. In this way people could see other people's faults as large as life, but could never observe their own faults.

Moral: This story illustrates the busybody who is blind to his own faults, but always concerns himself about other people's faults.

Advice is like snow

Advice is like snow.
The softer it falls, the easier it's absorbed, the deeper it sinks, and the longer it lasts.
    Author unknown

Giving criticism

Do not use a hatchet to remove a fly from your friend's forehead.
    Chinese proverb

Search others for their virtues, yourself for faults.
    Author unknown

Encouragement after censure is as the sun after a shower.
    Goethe

Some dos and don'ts about giving criticism

1. Choose an appropriate time.
2. Choose an appropriate place.
3. Be positive and acknowledge the positive. Say something good *before* you launch into critical mode.

4. Keep calm.
   Be like a duck, calm on the surface, but always paddling like the dickens underneath.
   Michael Caine
5. Be sympathetic, even empathize if you can manage it.
6. Be optimistic.
7. Don't go on about generalizations, be specific.
8. Better to correct someone openly than to let him think you don't care for him at all.
   Proverbs 28:13
9. Someone who holds back the truth causes trouble, but one who openly criticizes works for peace.
   Proverbs 10:10
10. Praise in public. Criticize in private.

Receiving criticism

Most of us would rather be ruined by praise than helped by criticism.
> **Author unknown**

Don't criticize your wife

You should never criticize your wife's judgment – look who she decided to marry!

Concluding thought

My idea of an agreeable person is a person who agrees with me.
> **Hugo Bohun**

Revenge and envy

Forgive friends

Write in the sand the flaws of your friend.
   Pythagoras

> ### So says the president
>
> ### Making friends
> Am I not destroying my enemies when I make friends of them?
>   Abraham Lincoln
>
> ### The cycle of hatred
> Always remember others may hate you but those who hate you don't win unless you hate them. And then you destroy yourself.
>   Richard M. Nixon
>
> ### Let the healing process start
> A tree takes a long time to grow, and wounds take a long time to heal, but we must begin.
>   Bill Clinton

A stiff apology

A stiff apology is a second insult.
   G.K. Chesterton

Insults

Sensible people will ignore an insult.
   Proverbs 12:16

Avenging insults

A smiling face, and forgiveness, are the best way to avenge an insult.
   Spanish proverb

Hatred

Hate is blind as well as love.
Author unknown

Human nature

It is human nature to hate the man you have hurt.
Tacitus

Hatred versus love

Hatred paralyses life; love releases it.
Hatred confuses life; love harmonizes it.
Hatred darkens life; love illuminates it.
Martin Luther King

Who never forgives?

The offender never forgives.
Russian proverb

Unclench your fist

You cannot shake hands with a clenched fist.
Indira Gandhi

Forgiving others

He that cannot forgive others breaks the bridge over which he must pass himself; for every man has need to be forgiven.
Thomas Fuller

Remembering being wronged

To be wronged is nothing unless you continue to remember it.
Confucius

I resolved

I resolved never to do anything out of revenge.
Jonathan Edwards

Envy

Envy is the greatest of all diseases among men.
Euripides

Gossip

St Augustine's warning

To guard against gossip Augustine had a notice displayed at his dinner table. It read like this: 'Let him who takes pleasure in mauling the lives of the absent know that his own is not such as to fit him to sit at this table.'

Augustine really meant business with this notice. On one occasion, when he was entertaining some close friends, the conversation began to infringe the prohibition. Augustine burst out and said, 'Either the notice will be removed, or I, your host, will retire to my cell and leave the feast.'

Three rules

The three essential rules when speaking of others are:
- Is it true?
- Is it kind?
- Is it necessary?

Author unknown

Listening to gossip is as bad as passing on gossip

Those who talk about others to us will talk about us to others.

Author unknown

Without gossip

Without wood, a fire goes out; without gossip, quarrelling stops.

Proverbs 26:20

Busyness

Barrenness

Beware of the barrenness of a busy life.

Extreme busyness

Extreme busyness, whether at school or college, kirk or market, is a symptom of deficient vitality.
   Robert Louis Stevenson

Seeming to do is not doing

Being busy does not always mean real work.
The object of all work is production or accomplishment and to either of these ends there must be forethought, system, planning, intelligence and honest purpose, as well as perspiration.
Seeming to do is not doing.
   Thomas Alva Edison

Little busyness

Great peace is found in little busyness.
   Geoffrey Chaucer

Stay busy

The secret to a long life is to stay busy, get plenty of exercise and don't drink too much. Then again, don't drink too little.
   Hermann Smith-Johannson, 103-year-old cross-country skier

The pitfall of being too busy

Never get so busy making a living that you forget to make a life.
   Anonymous

Overweight and underweight

Gluttony kills

Gluttony kills more than the sword.
   Latin proverb

Overeating

More people die from overeating than from undernourishment.
   The Talmud

Breakfast is the most important meal

For a long life, breakfast like a king, lunch moderately and dine like a pauper.
   Author unknown

You are what you eat

Man is what he eats.
   German proverb

Bulimia – the bingeing disorder

According to the Institute of Psychiatry in London and Boston University, between 1988 and 1993 the number of people suffering from bulimia went up threefold from 15 out of every 100,000 to 50 out of every 100,000.

Dr Janet Treasure of the Institute of Psychiatry said that the increase had 'to do with the culture of thinness and weight-watching ... It's also a way people now find of expressing distress ... people feel they need to solve all their problems themselves and they develop bulimia as a way of dealing with them.'

A few facts about losing weight

1. Exercise
Contrary to popular belief exercise is not a brilliant way to lose weight – although it is good in other ways. To lose one pound of body fat you need to walk about 80 kilometres – that's about 50 miles.

2. Cutting down on calories
Cutting down on calories is a much better way to lose weight. Sugar only gives you calories, and foods that contain sugar have a very high calorific value, so try to cut down on them.

3. Bring on the vegetables
Replace foods containing sugar with vegetables, wholemeal bread and fruit.

4. Counting the calories
Overweight people take in about 2,500 a day.
Aim for 1,500 calories a day, bearing in mind that 3,500 calories equals one pound of body fat.

5. Think of losing weight as a long-term process
If you lose weight very quickly, you are likely to put it all back on again quite soon. Aim to lose two pounds a week. This would give you a weight loss of one stone (6.3 kg) in seven weeks.

6. High calories
Foods with high calories are:

food	calories per 100 gm portion
Peanut butter	620
Roasted peanuts	570
Butter	740
Margarine	730
Streaky bacon, fried	500

7. Low calories
Foods with low calories are:

food	calories per 100 gm portion
Boiled cabbage	10
Brussel sprouts	20
Baked beans	60
Cooked porridge	45
Chicken noodle soup	20
Tomatoes	15

Overcoming problems

part four

Enhancing your Positive Qualities

Leadership

So says the president
The best executive

The best executive is the one who has sense enough to pick good men to do what he wants done, and selfrestraint enough to keep from meddling with them while they do it.
   Theodore Roosevelt

Learning from proverbs

Many hands make light work.
   Proverb

Two heads are better than one.
   Proverb

Richard Hoptroff

Computer buffs need no introduction to Richard Hoptroff. He's the man who made millions from his computer programme *4Thought* which accurately predicted the end of the recession in the British economy.

His recipe for success? Delegate.

'Too many people in the software business work too hard. Not me. If someone can do a job better than me, I'll hire him to do it.'
   Richard Hoptroff

Too much talk

Many attempts to communicate are nullified by saying too much.
   Robert Greenleaf, Director of Management Research, AT&T

Rarer than ability

There is something rarer than ability. It is the ability to recognize ability.
   Elbert Hubbard

Enhancing your positive qualities

Three steps to effective leadership

1. 'Give a man a fish,
and you feed him for a day.'

2. 'Teach a man how to fish
and you feed him for a lifetime.'

3. The above two steps are well known. But 'step three' is less well known.
'Train teachers of fishermen.'
This will result in all of society being affected.

Managing by wandering around

Leadership can be based on the MBWA principle: Managing by Wandering Around.

To 'wander' with customers is to be in touch with the first vibrations of the new.

Leadership

Enthusiasm

Enthusiasm is a two-edged sword

If you aren't fired with enthusiasm, you will be fired with enthusiasm.

Vince Lombardi

The necessity of enthusiasm

Nothing great was every achieved without enthusiasm ... Every great movement in the annals of history is the triumph of enthusiasm.

Ralph Waldo Emerson, *Essays, Circles*

Types of effort

Forced effort tires us three times as fast as enthusiastic effort. One of life's richest blessings is doing what comes naturally.

Author unknown

Five steps to an enthusiastic life

1. Stop deprecating yourself.
2. Stop thinking about yourself all the time.
3. Recall the words of Goethe: 'He who has a firm will moulds the world to himself.'
4. Have an overriding goal in your life.

    The purpose of medicine is to prevent significant disease, to decrease pain and to postpone death when it is meaningful to do so. Technology has to support these goals. If not, it may even be counterproductive.

    Dr Joel J. Nobel, co-founder, Emergency Care Research Institute
5. Stop wasting your mental energy on complaining.

    Grumbling is the death of love.

    Marlene Dietrich

Practise it

To have enthusiasm, practise it.

Think of young children

Observing small children one will conclude that their outstanding characteristic is enthusiasm. They think that the world is fantastic. Everything fascinates them.

'The secret of genius is to carry the spirit of the child into old age,' said Thomas Huxley.

A truism to ponder

What is required is sight and insight – then you might add one more: excite.
   Robert Frost

Security is not an alternative

Life is either a daring adventure or nothing at all. Security is mostly a superstition. It does not exist in nature.
   Helen Keller

There is no such thing as security. There never has been.
   Germaine Greer

Habits

> ### Greek wisdom
>
> ### We are ...
>
> We are what we repeatedly do.
> Excellence, then, is not an act, but a habit.
> Aristotle
>
> ### Who is the braver?
>
> I count him braver who conquers his desires than him who conquers his enemies; for the hardest victory is the victory over self.
> Aristotle

Reformation required

Nothing so needs reforming as other people's habits.
Mark Twain

Change yourself!

Everyone thinks of changing the world, but no one thinks of changing himself.
Leo Tolstoy

Good and bad habits

Good habits are hard to acquire but easy to live with.
Bad habits are easy to acquire but hard to live with.
Author unknown

Threads into ropes

Habits begin like threads in a spider's web, but end up like ropes.
Spanish proverb

Overcoming habit

Habit is overcome by habit.
Thomas à Kempis

Principles

Advice from an actress

You must learn
day by day,
year by year,
to broaden your horizon.
The more things you love,
the more you are interested in,
the more you enjoy,
the more you are indignant about,
the more you have left when anything happens.
   Ethel Barrymore

So says the president

In matters of principle, stand like a rock;
in matters of taste, swim with the current.
   Thomas Jefferson

The power is in the principles

'The power is in the principles' is the slogan of many of the self-help books published in the '90s.

The choice is between a clock and a compass

We are not in control of our lives; *principles* are. This idea provides a key insight into the frustration people have had with the traditional 'time management' approach to life.

This approach to running our lives has been likened to a *clock*, as we time how we live each part of our day, endeavouring to make it more and more efficient. Rather than offering you another clock, the *principle* approach to running our lives provides us with a *compass*.

There is something more important than knowing how fast you are going – we need to know where we are going.

It's much more a matter of what you do and why you do it, than how fast you get it done.

Enhance your communications

Here are ten pointers to ponder over about how to communicate effectively. These ten pointers assume that you already have a goal in mind.

Make sure that you have a desired outcome. Before you make a business call or go to a business meeting decide on your desired outcome. Then focus on how to make it easy for the other party to give it to you.

1. *What you say to yourself at work.*
   Everything you say to yourself either helps you or hinders you.
   Do you say to yourself, 'I can do it', or do you say to yourself, 'I can't do it'.
   Positive self talk can transform your day.
2. *Cut out unnecessary non-communicating speech fillers.*
   These are 'words' such as 'it's a bit like, urrrh, ummmm, weeeell'. The more you use these 'words' the less people will listen to what you want to communicate.
3. *Never dilute or contradict what you are trying to say.*
   Avoid the word 'but' in your sentences. Replace 'but' with 'and'. To exaggerate is to dilute.
4. *Don't take NO for an answer.*
   Remember, 'no' means 'negotiate'.
5. *Map out what you want to say in advance.*
   Don't go into a meeting or a conversation with your mouth at full throttle and your mind out of gear.
6. *Maximize silences*
   Pauses, especially between sentences and before you give a reply, can be a very powerful way of gaining the full concentration of the people you are talking with.
7. *Speak up*
   Don't worry about what kind of reception your words may have.
   Don't stop yourself asking questions.

Don't deliberately withhold compliments where they are appropriate.

Don't be scared of making comments on things.

8. *If you want something, ask for it.*
9. *Remember: body language is important.*

    Body language accounts for much more than the words you use.

    For example, think about how you stand. Do you have a habit of:
    - crossing your legs
    - folding your arms
    - leaning against something as you speak?

    All these things reduce the impact of what you are trying to communicate.

    A more positive way to stand is:
    - Have both of your feet on the ground
    - Do not tilt your head
    - Stand tall and straight
    - Do not cross your legs or feet.

10. *Have you ever considered how your voice projects?*

    Don't let your voice become shrill ... even if you are angry or upset. That will be read as a sign of weakness.

    Don't speak from your throat but from your diaphragm, as singers are trained to do.

    Don't whisper. Speak so everyone can easily hear what you are saying.

    Don't forget to breathe! Take frequent, deep breaths as you speak.

Receiving strength from others

> **Eastern wisdom**
>
> Behind an able man there are always other able men.
>   Chinese proverb

Learn from others

Learn all you can from others. The school of experience takes so long that the graduates are too old to go to work.
  Henry Ford

Dale Carnegie

Dale Carnegie (1888–1955), born in Maryville, Missouri, started out as a travelling salesman. He began teaching public speaking at a New York YMCA in 1912. His book, *Art of Public Speaking*, was published in 1915. He became a well-known public speaker, and a pioneer in personality development, eventually teaching private courses and creating a chain of schools. He is perhaps best known for his 1936 book *How to Win Friends and Influence People*, which has sold over 10 million copies in 30 languages.

My ideas are borrowed ones

The ideas I stand for are not mine.
I borrowed them from Socrates.
I swiped them from Chesterfield.
I stole them from Jesus.
And I put them in a book.
  Dale Carnegie

Many advisers

Many advisers mean security.
    Proverbs 11:14

Brotherhood

Live alone and free, like a tree, but in the brotherhood of the forest.

> Slogan daubed on the Berlin Wall, which was breached on 8 November 1989, and then broken down.

Learning from proverbs

Many things are lost for want of asking.
> Old English proverb

There is an art in asking

1. Overcome the things which prevent you from asking.
   Defeat the fear of being turned down.
2. Plan how you are going to make your request.
   Ask artfully.
3. Never beg.
4. Never demand.
   A proverb from Madagascar goes, 'The dog's bark is not might, but fright.'
5. Make the request.
   Don't be scared of asking.

Contentment

Greek wisdom

He is richest who is content with the least, for content is the wealth of nature.
   Socrates

Aesop's fables

The town-mouse and the country-mouse

The country-mouse invited a friend who lived in a town house to have a meal with him in the country. The friend accepted at once. But when he found that the meal consisted only of barley and other corn, he said to his host, 'Let me tell you, my friend, you live like an ant. But I have so many good things to eat, and if you come to my home I will share them all with you.'

So the country-mouse set off with the town-mouse to his home. The town-mouse showed his friend his beans and peas, bread, dates, cheese, honey, and fruit. The country-mouse was amazed to see all this lovely food and congratulated the town-mouse and cursed his own lot. Just as they were about to start their meal the door opened, and the timid creatures were so frightened by what they heard that they ran for their holes in the floor. When they returned and were just about to tuck into some dried figs, they saw someone else coming into the room to collect something, and once more had to dive for cover. The country-mouse decided that he would go home, even though he was still hungry.
'Goodbye, my friend,' he said, with a groan. 'You may eat until you are full and enjoy yourself. But your good food costs you dear in terms of danger and fear. I prefer to gnaw my poor meals of barley and corn without any fear or having to constantly keep on the watch for an intruder.'

Moral: A simple life with peace and quiet is better than eating the finest foods and being in the grip of fear.

Contentment and cheerfulness

Cheerfulness and content are great beautifiers and are famous preservers of youthful looks.
   Charles Dickens

Which way to look

To be content, look backward on those who possess less than yourself, not forward on those who possess more.
   Benjamin Franklin, *Poor Richard's Almanac*

Today

As yesterday is history, and tomorrow may never come, I have resolved from this day on, I will do all the business I can honestly, have all the fun I can reasonably, do all the good I can willingly, and save my digestion by thinking pleasantly.
   Robert Louis Stevenson

Cineas and Pyrrhus

Cineas was trying to stop Pyrrhus from attacking the Romans, and said, 'Sir, when you have conquered them, what will you do next?'

Pyrrhus replied, 'I will conquer Sicily, as it is an easy target.'

'What will you do after Sicily is conquered?' asked Cineas.

'Why, then, I will go on to Africa and take Carthage, ' replied Pyrrhus enthusiastically.

'After you have conquered all this, what will you do then?' persisted Cineas.

'We will then take Greece and take back everything we have lost there, ' answered Pyrrhus.

'When you have conquered everyone, what benefits do you expect to derive from all your victories?' asked Cineas.

'Then we will be able to settle down and enjoy ourselves.'

'Sir!' said Cineas, 'May we not do this now? You already possess a kingdom of your own. He who cannot enjoy himself with a kingdom will not be satisfied with the whole world.'

The greatest wealth

Health is the greatest gift, contentment the greatest wealth, faithfulness the best relationship.
   Buddha

Genius

The essence of genius

The essence of genius is knowing what to overlook.
   William James

Taking pains

Genius is an infinite capacity for taking pains.
   Author unknown

Genius is not enough

Genius usually starts great things; only labour and drudgery finish them.
   Author unknown

Mr Paderewski

Queen Victoria: 'Mr Paderewski, you are a genius.'
Paderewski: 'That may be, Ma'am, but before I was a genius, I was a drudge.'
   Paderewski the violin player who often practised the same phrase on his violin 50 times to perfect it

Inspiration and perspiration

Genius is one per cent inspiration and 99 per cent perspiration.
   Thomas Edison

Patience

Genius is nothing but a great aptitude for being patient.
   Buffon

Originality

The principal mark of genius is not perfection but originality, the opening of new frontiers.
   Arthur Koestler

Crying

A therapy

Crying is therapeutic.

Men and women crying

Men cry on average between two and ten times a year. Women cry an average of nine to thirty times a year.

I wept not

I wept not, so to stone I grew within.
   Dante

Tears and the soul

What soap is for the body, tears are for the soul.
   Jewish proverb

The good and tears

The good are always prone to tears.
   Greek proverb

Crying and grief

To weep is to make less the depth of grief.
   William Shakespeare

Tears soften down the temper

'It [weeping] opens the lungs, washes the countenance, exercises the eyes, and softens down the temper, ' said Mr Bumble. 'So cry away.'
   Charles Dickens, *Oliver Twist*

Tears and laughter

Those who don't know how to weep with their whole heart don't know how to laugh either.
   Golda Meir

Risk-taking

Anyone for champagne?

Adventure is the champagne of life.
   G.K. Chesterton

Great deeds

Great deeds are usually wrought at great risk.
He who doesn't risk never gets to drink champagne.
   Russian proverb

Poet's corner

Like chessmen

Daring ideas are like chessmen moved forward. They may be beaten, but they may start a winning game.
   Goethe

Being a conformist

No one can possibly achieve any real and lasting success or 'get rich' in business by being a conformist.
   J. Paul Getty

Boldness

Whatever you can do, or believe you can, begin it.
Boldness has genius, power and magic in it.
   Goethe

A fact to ponder

Walt Disney was regarded as a pioneer, entrepreneur and risk-taker in the film-making industry. He was made bankrupt six times, persevered and died a rich man.

Don't worry about failing

It's nobler to try something and fail than to try nothing and succeed. The result may be the same, but you won't be. We always grow more through defeats than victories.
   Author unknown

Regard failure as feedback.
Do not be afraid about taking risks.

Safety first?

The desire for safety stands against every great and noble enterprise.
   Tacitus

Risks and failure

If your life is free of failures, you're not taking enough risks.

Positive attitudes towards life

Be bold
Fortune favours the bold.
   Virgil

Life is dangerous
He that will not sail till all dangers are over must never put to sea.
   Thomas Fuller

Fear less, hope more
   Fear less, hope more,
   eat less, chew more,
   whine less, breathe more,
   talk less, say more,
   hate less, love more,
   and all good things will be yours.
   Swedish proverb

Joys and troubles
Man only likes to count his troubles, but he does not count his joys.
   Fyodor Dostoyevsky

Looking at the wrong door
When one door closes another door opens; but we so often look so long and so regretfully upon the closed door, that we do not see the ones which open for us.
   Alexander Graham Bell

Take giant steps
Don't be afraid to take big steps. You can't cross a chasm in two small jumps.
   David Lloyd George

Smile

Smile at each other, smile at your wife, smile at your husband, smile at your children, smile at each other – it doesn't matter who it is – and that will help you to grow up in greater love for each other.
   Mother Teresa

Learning from Mahatma Gandhi

I claim to be no more than an average man with less than average abilities. I have not the shadow of a doubt that any man or woman can achieve what I have, if he or she would make the same effort and cultivate the same hope and faith.

Looking for fruit all the time

It's the action, not the fruit of the action, that's important. You have to do the right thing. It may not be in your power, it may not be in your time, that there'll be any fruit. But that doesn't mean you stop doing the right thing. You may never know what results come from your action. But if you do nothing, there will be no result.

Live and pray

Live among men as if the eye of God were upon you; pray to God as if men were listening to you.
   Seneca

When you arise

When you arise in the morning, think of what a precious privilege it is to be alive – to breathe, to think, to enjoy, to love.
   Marcus Aurelius

The limitation of competition

Learn to create, not compete.

Attitude to suffering

Pain is inevitable.
Suffering is optional.
    Anonymous

Sing a song

Those who wish to sing always find a song.
    Swedish proverb

Living well

The most fruitful of all the arts is the art of living well.
    Cicero

The brevity of life

Life is too short to be little.
    Benjamin Disraeli

Count your blessings

Concentrate on what you have.

Determination

Opportunity knocks

If you don't hear opportunity knocking, find another door.
    Anonymous

Objections

Nothing will ever be attempted, if all possible objections must be first overcome.
    Samuel Johnson, *Rasselas*

Don't let opposition put you down

Great spirits will always encounter violent opposition from mediocre people.
    Albert Einstein

Keep trying

It is my firm belief that I have a link with the past and a responsibility to the future. I cannot give up. I cannot despair. There's a whole future, generations to come. I have to keep trying.
    King Hussein of Jordan

Keep fighting

You may have to fight a battle more than once to win it.
    Margaret Thatcher

A positive view of failure

We haven't failed. We now know a thousand things that won't work, so we're that much closer to finding what will.
    Thomas Edison, after hundreds of abortive experiments trying to produce a lightbulb

Enduring

Nothing great was ever done without much enduring.
    Catherine of Siena

Hard work and success

Fun or drudgery

Work is either fun or drudgery. It depends on your attitude. I like fun.
Colleen C. Barrett

Prepare

Before everything else, getting ready is the secret of success.
Henry Ford

800,000 hours

It took computers 800,000 hours to render the final animation of the film *Toy Story*. Woody's mouth has 58 variables on the computer.

Time in the office

No one on their deathbed says, 'I should have spent more time at the office.'
Barbara Walters

All your strength and soul

Only one who devotes himself to a cause with his whole strength and soul can be a true master. For this reason mastery demands all of a person.
Albert Einstein

Do what you can

Let us be content, in work,
To do the thing we can, and not presume
To fret because it's so little.
Elizabeth Barrett Browning

A formula for success?

If A equals success, then the formula is A equals X plus Y plus Z.
X is work.
Y is play.
Z is keep your mouth shut.
   Albert Einstein

Success and work

The dictionary is the only place that success comes before work.
   Anonymous

Uphill

There are many roads to success – but they are all uphill.

The men I have seen succeed

The men I have seen succeed
   have always been cheerful and hopeful,
   who went about their business with a smile on their faces,
   and took the changes and chances to this mortal life like men.
   If you wish to be miserable,
      you must think about yourself;
      about what you want,
      what you like,
      what respect people ought to pay you,
      what people think of you,
      and then to you nothing will be pure.
You will spoil everything you touch; you will make sin and misery out of everything God sends you;
you can be as wretched as you choose.
   Charles Kingsley

Listening

Effective communication

Listening is as important as talking in effective communication.

A sympathetic ear

There is no greater loan than a sympathetic ear.
   Anonymous

Listening – essential for communicators

We spend about 80% of waking moments in communicating with others. Out of this time, 45% is spent in listening to others.

Give yourself a listening test

Question 1: Which best describes your listening abilities?
   Dreadful
   Poor
   Average
   Above average
   Excellent
   Superior to most other people

Question 2: On a scale of 0–100, how would you rate how you used your own listening skills in the past week?

Question 3: On a scale of 0–100, how would the following people rate you as a listener?
   Your partner?
   Your best friend?
   Your boss?
   The people you manage at work?

When a woman talks

When a woman is talking to you, listen to what she says with her eyes.
   Victor Hugo

Enhancing your positive qualities

Most people never listen
When people talk, listen completely. Most people never listen.

The wise person
The wise man has long ears and a short tongue.
   German proverb

Two ears, one mouth
God gave a man two ears and only one mouth.
Why don't we listen twice as much as we talk?
   Chinese proverb

Listening and learning
Blessed are those who listen, for they shall learn.
   Author unknown

Barriers to listening
1. Daydreaming.
2. Thinking about what you are about to say.
3. Relating what you hear to yourself.
   'Yes, my children are much better behaved than that.'
4. Labelling other people, rather than listening to what they are saying.
5. Being too quick to offer advice.
6. Making no room for being sympathetic.
   'It'll work out better next time, maybe.'
7. Selective listening; just listening to bits of the conversation that appeal to you.

We grow by becoming listeners
Growth always comes when we listen to our critics.

First steps
The first step in becoming a listener is to learn to ask questions.

Failure need not be final

The key to failure

I don't know the key to success, but the key to failure is trying to please everybody.
  Bill Cosby

Failure is not fatal

Success is not final, failure is not fatal: it is the courage to continue that counts.
  Winston Churchill

Failure and opportunity

Failure is only the opportunity to begin again more intelligently.
  Henry Ford

A lesson in humility

In God's economy, nothing is wasted. Through failure, we learn a lesson in humility which is probably needed, painful though it is.
  William Wilson, co-founder of Alcoholics Anonymous

So says the president

To fail can be heroic

It is not the critic who counts; not the man who points out how the strong man stumbled or where the doer of deeds could have done them better. The credit belongs to the man who is actually in the arena; whose face is marred by dust and sweat and blood; who strives valiantly; who errs and comes short again and again; who knows the great enthusiasms, the great devotions, and spends himself in a worthy cause; who, at the best, knows the triumph of high achievement; and who, at the worst, if he fails, at least fails while daring greatly, so that his place shall never be with those cold and timid souls who knew neither victory nor defeat.
  Theodore Roosevelt

Choosing

Free to choose

You are free to choose, but the choices you make today will determine what you will have, what you will be, and what you will do in the tomorrow of your life.

Zig Zigler

The urgency addiction

The enemy of the best is the good.

Each choice you make

Every time you make a choice, you are turning the central part of you, the part that chooses, into something a little different from what it was before.

C.S. Lewis

1. **A choice about speaking about your health**
   What we choose to talk about has a lot to do with our health.
   The more we choose to talk about how ill we are, the sicker we become.
   The choice is ours. It's really all about the attitude we have to life.
2. **A choice about short-term and long-term aims**
   Every day we choose between long-term goals or immediate gratification.
3. **A choice between good and evil**
   Nearly all our choices either support good or support evil.

Understanding and surviving

Understanding ourselves

Everything that irritates us about others can lead us to an understanding of ourselves.
    Carl Jung

How to treat people

Treat people as if they were what they ought to be and you help them become what they are capable of being.
    Goethe

Understanding adversity

Adversity reveals
Adversity reveals genius,
prosperity conceals it.
    Horace

Adversity introduces
Adversity introduces a man to himself.
    Anonymous

Think of a kite
A kite flies against the wind.
The stronger the wind, the higher the kite flies.

When the sea is calm
Anyone can hold the helm when the sea is calm.
    Publius Syrus

So says the president

Crisis

When written in Chinese, the word 'crisis' is composed of two characters.
One represents danger and the other represents opportunity.
    John F. Kennedy

Viktor Frankl

Viktor Frankl, an Austrian psychologist who survived the death camps of Nazi Germany, made a significant discovery. As he found within himself the capacity to rise above his humiliating circumstances, he became an observer as well as a participant in the experience. He watched others who shared the ordeal. He was intrigued with the question of what made it possible for some people to survive when most died.

He looked at several factors – health, vitality, family structure, intelligence, survival skills. Finally, he concluded that none of these factors was primarily responsible.

The single most significant factor, he realized, was a sense of future vision.

Frankl explained this as 'the impelling conviction of those who were to survive that they had a mission to perform, some important work left to do.'

The last of the human freedoms

We who lived in concentration camps can remember the men who walked through the huts comforting others, giving away their last piece of bread. They offer sufficient proof that everything can be taken from a man but one thing: the last of the human freedoms – to choose one's attitude in any given set of circumstances, to choose one's own way.

Viktor Frankl

Understanding and surviving

Mind over matter

Success in 'no hope' situations

Most of the important things in the world have been accomplished by people who have kept on trying when there seemed to be no help at all.

Dale Carnegie

> ### So says the president
> **It's all in the mind**
>
> Most people are about as happy as they make up their minds to be.
>
> Abraham Lincoln

Indecision

There is no more miserable human being than one in whom nothing is habitual but indecision.

Herodotus

Two steps to achieve mind over matter

1. Think.
2. Change the way you think.

I never change my mind or anything else

Only the wisest and the stupidest of men never change.

Confucius

Are you the same as you were ten years ago?

The man who views the world at 50 the same as he did at 20 has wasted 30 years of his life.

Muhammad Ali

How are your wrinkles?

The face is the index of the mind.
> Latin proverb

CDTs

Dr John A. Schindler has claimed that thousands of people are suffering from an illness which he calls 'CDTs':
- cares
- difficulties
- troubles.

Another name for it is psychosomatic illness – the effect on the body of mental states.

Mind over matter in sport

Your body only follows your mind.
> Glenn Hoddle, coach to England's football team, explaining why he believes that the mental attitude of his team is more important than their physical fitness.

The power of positive thinking

The power of positive thinking is stronger in fighting disease than all of the technology of modern medicine.

Unqualified

The bulk of mankind is as well qualified for flying as for thinking.
> Jonathan Swift

Living with hope

The gleaming taper's light

Hope, like the gleaming taper's light,
Adorns and cheers our way;
And still, as darker grows the night,
Emits a brighter ray.
   Oliver Goldsmith

Giving people hope

Over 20 years ago Jean Vanier invited two severely handicapped people to live with him in a small house in a French village. With very little money, they shared everything together: shopping, cleaning, cooking. That was the beginning of L'Arche communities in which able-bodied people live alongside handicapped people. Today there are 106 communities worldwide.

At a meeting in London, Vanier described a young man of 26, who could do nothing for himself, and had to be fed through his stomach. The assistants who lived with him said, 'Antonio has transformed our lives. He has brought us from a world of competitiveness to a world of tenderness and mutuality'; 'He had a power of deep communion, not through the head but through the heart.'

Vanier told Ysenda Maxtone Graham, 'The real reason L'Arche has worked is the incredible beauty of people with disabilities.'

A waking dream

Hope is a waking dream.
   Aristotle

Totally without hope ...

Totally without hope one cannot live.
To live without hope is to cease to live.
Hell is hopelessness.
   Fyodor Dostoyevsky

Patience

The weak and the strong
The weak man is impetuous, the strong is patient.
   Proverb

The queen of the virtues
Patience is the queen of virtues.
   John Chrysostom

Patience's achievement
Our patience will achieve more than our force.
   Edmund Burke

Waiting
All things come to those who wait.
   Proverb

Her pace is patience
Great haste makes great waste.
Adopt the pace of nature.
Her pace is patience.
   Author unknown

Patience and perseverance
Patience and perseverance have a magical effect before which difficulties disappear and obstacles vanish.
   John Quincy Adams

A handful of patience
A handful of patience is worth a bushel of brains.
   Dutch proverb

part five

Helping Others

Compassion

Learning from an 11-year-old

In 1983, when he was 11 years old, Trevor Farrel saw a television programme about the plight of homeless people in Philadelphia, about 18 miles from his home. He persuaded his parents to drive there with a blanket and pillow to give to a homeless person. Each night after that they drove into the city, until they had nothing left to give away.

Then Trevor advertised the needs of the homeless in Philadelphia and asked for gifts of old blankets, pillows and warm clothes.

His story was taken up by a television station and a newspaper. So many gifts came in that a warehouse had to be found to hold everything. A church gave a shelter with 33 rooms, which they called 'Trevor's Place', and within two years 250 people had joined Trevor and his parents each night to serve hot meals to the homeless.

> Compassion is the basis for all morality.
> Arthur Schopenhauer

Refugees

Eleanor Roosevelt (1884–1962), fought for refugees after the Second World War and helped to ensure that they would not be forgotten when the UN Charter was written. She wrote: 'If civilization is to survive, we must cultivate the science of human relationships – the ability of all people of all kinds to live together and work together in the same world, at peace.'

Charity can be harmful

Charity degrades those who receive it and hardens those who dispense it.
George Sand, *Consuelo*

Charity is injurious unless it helps the recipient to become independent of it.
John D. Rockefeller

Helping yourself as you help others

The best way to cheer yourself up is to try to cheer somebody else up.
    Mark Twain

Compassion is in season

Love is a fruit in season at all times, and within reach of every hand.
    Mother Teresa

Doing a little

Nobody makes a greater mistake than he who does nothing because he could only do a little.
    Edmund Burke

Do what you can – now

Our grand business is not to see what lies dimly at a distance, but to do what lies clearly at hand.
    Thomas Carlyle

Actions versus knowledge

The great end in life is not knowledge but action.
    T.H. Huxley

A spirit of compassion

I believe that man will not merely endure. He will prevail. He is immortal, not because he alone among creatures has an inexhaustible voice, but because he has a soul, a spirit capable of compassion and sacrifice and endurance.
    William Faulkner, acceptance speech for his 1949 Nobel Prize for Literature

Service

> ### So says the president
> **Do what you can**
>
> Do what you can,
> with what you have,
> where you are.
>   Theodore Roosevelt

Service can be judged by four questions

When at some future date the high court of history sits in judgment on each one of us recording whether in our brief span of service we fulfilled our responsibilities to the state, our success or failure, in whatever office we may hold, will be measured by the answers to four questions.

1. Were we truly men of courage?
2. Were we truly men of judgment?
3. Were we truly men of integrity?
4. Were we truly men of dedication?

  John F. Kennedy, when president-elect, to the Massachusetts legislature

Two truisms to ponder

Service is the virtue that distinguished the great of all times and which they will be remembered by.
  Bryant S. Hinkley, one of the early pioneers of the American West

The service we render to others is really the rent we pay for our room on this earth.
  Author unknown

Advice from Russia

The vocation of every man and woman is to serve other people.
  Leo Tolstoy

Joy can be real only if people look upon their life as a service, and have a definite object in life outside themselves and their personal happiness.
  Leo Tolstoy

Service and leadership

I declare before you all that my whole life, whether it be long or short, shall be devoted to your service and the service of our great imperial family to which we all belong.
  Queen Elizabeth II, her twenty-first birthday address

Service is our duty

I believe that the rendering of useful service is the common duty of mankind and that only in the purifying fire of sacrifice is the dross of selfishness consumed and the greatness of the human soul set free.
  John D. Rockefeller Jr, 'Credo', engraved in the plaza of the Rockefeller Center

Students and public service

There are many other possibilities more enlightening than the struggle to become the local doctor's most affluent ulcer case.
  Nelson A. Rockefeller, Governor of New York, encouraging Syracuse University graduates to enter public service

The purpose of education

The ability to think straight, some knowledge of the past, some vision of the future, some skill to do useful service, some urge to fit that service into the well-being of the community – these are the most vital things education must try to produce.
  Virginian Gildersleeve, Dean Emeritus of Barnard College, USA

Positive attitudes towards others

Appreciation

Appreciation is a wonderful thing: it makes what is excellent in others belong to us as well.
   Voltaire

How we view people

Our attitude to all people would be Christian if we regarded them as though they were dying, and determined our relation to them in the light of death, both of their death and of our own.
   Nicolas Berdyaev

The Beatitudes

The Beatitudes: Beautiful Attitudes
   Author unknown

Blessed is ...

Happy are those who know they are spiritually poor;
   the Kingdom of heaven belongs to them!
Happy are those who mourn;
   God will comfort them!
Happy are those who are humble;
   they will receive what God has promised!
Happy are those whose greatest desire is to do what God requires;
   God will satisfy them fully!
Happy are those who are merciful to others;
   God will be merciful to them!
Happy are the pure in heart;
   they will see God!
Happy are those who work for peace;
   God will call them his children!
   Matthew 5:3–9

Form a human link

Go beyond 'me' to 'we'. Forge a human connection.

Never despise anyone

Throughout our life, our worst weaknesses and meannesses are usually committed for the sake of the people whom we most despise.

   Charles Dickens, *Great Expectations*

Attitude to inferiors

Behave to your inferiors as you would wish your betters to behave to you.

   Seneca, *Epistles*

Beware of the 'conditional reflex' to people

The Russian neuro-psychologist, Professor Pavlov, gave his whole life over to studying human behaviour.

His most famous experiment involved a number of dogs which were used to demonstrate the conditioned reflex. Pavlov had noticed how dogs produce saliva as soon as they are shown food. Pavlov proceeded to ring a bell just before he fed the dogs in this experiment. It wasn't long before Pavlov could ring the bell and the dogs started to salivate, whether or not they received food.

Pavlov went on to repeat this experiment in two other ways: he shone a light just before the dogs were fed, and he touched the dogs' bodies in the same spot just before they were fed. Once again the dogs produced saliva each time the light shone or whenever they were touched, irrespective of whether they were fed. From these observations Pavlov developed his theory of the conditioned reflex.

How far you go in life

How far you go in life depends on your being tender with the young, compassionate with the aged, sympathetic with the striving, and tolerant of the weak and strong. Because someday in your life you will have been all of these.

   George Washington Carver

> **So says the president**
>
> ### Leadership
> Leadership is the art of getting someone else to do something you want done because he wants to do it.
>   Dwight D. Eisenhower

Learning the art of effective delegation
Our company never really expanded until I realized, through a nervous breakdown, that I couldn't do everything myself. So I learned to work through others and our business boomed.
   F.W. Woolworth

If you don't know – be quiet
It is better to be silent, and be thought a fool, than to speak and remove all doubt.
   Silvan Engel

Being a channel of peace

An instrument of peace

Lord, make me a channel of your peace:
> where there is hatred,
> may I bring love;
> where there is wrong,
> may I bring the spirit of forgiveness;
> where there is discord,
> may I bring harmony;
> where there is error,
> may I bring truth;
> where there is doubt,
> may I bring hope;
> where there are shadows,
> may I bring light;
> where there is sadness,
> may I bring joy.

Lord, grant that I may seek rather to comfort than to be comforted;
> rather to understand than to be understood;
>> rather to love than to be loved,

for it is in forgetting myself that I find:
it is by forgiving that I am forgiven.

Francis of Assisi

Concluding thought

Will a person gain anything if he wins the whole world but loses his life? Of course not! There is nothing he can give to regain his life.

Matthew 16:26

Bringing up children

The first eight years

Give us the child for eight years and it will be a Bolshevik for ever.
    Lenin, to the Commissars of Education in Moscow, 1923

Early influences

Give me the children until they are seven and anyone may have them afterwards.

[Another version] Give us the child, and we will give you the man.
    Francis Xavier

Train up a child

Train up a child in the way he should go,
and when he is old he will not depart from it.
    Proverbs 22:6 (*RSV*)

Messengers

Every child comes with the message that God is not yet discouraged with Mankind.
    Rabindranath Tagore

Twelve rules for spoiling a child

1. Begin at infancy to give the child everything he wants.
   In this way he will grow up to believe that the world owes him a living.
2. When he picks up bad words laugh at him.
   This will make him think he's cute.
3. Never give him any spiritual training.
   Wait until he is 21 and then let him decide for himself.
4. Avoid the use of the word 'wrong'.
   The child may develop a guilt complex. This will condition him to believe later, when arrested for stealing a car, that society is against him and that he's being persecuted.

5. Pick up everything he leaves lying around: books, shoes, clothes.
   Do everything for him so that he will be experienced in throwing all responsibility on other people.
6. Let him read any printed material he can get his hands on.
   Be careful that his silverware and drinking glasses are sterilized, but let his mind feed on garbage.
7. Quarrel frequently in the presence of your children.
   In this way they will not be too shocked when the home is broken up later.
8. Give a child all the spending money he wants.
   Never let him earn his own.
   Why should he have things as tough as you had them?
9. Satisfy every craving for food, drink and comfort.
   See that every sensual desire is satisfied.
   Denial may lead to harmful frustration.
10. Take his part against neighbours, teachers, policemen.
    They are all prejudicial against your child.
11. When he gets into real trouble apologize for him.
    Say, 'I never could do anything with him.'
12. Prepare for a life of grief.
    You will be likely to have it.
    Issued by the Police Department of Houston, Texas

Planning for a lifetime

If you are planning for a year, sow rice; if you are planning for a decade, plant trees; if you are planning for a lifetime, educate people.
   Chinese proverb

Three old-fashioned virtues

Virtue

Virtue is stronger than a battering ram.
   Latin proverb

Good and evil

You call evil good and good evil. You turn darkness into light and light into darkness. You make what is bitter sweet, and what is sweet you make bitter.
   Isaiah 5:20

> ### Greek wisdom
> #### A gentle person
> He who is gentle remembers good rather than evil, the good one has received rather than the good one has done.
>   Aristotle

1. Gentleness

Show a gentle attitude towards everyone.
   Philippians 4:5

Gentleness and strength

Nothing is so strong as gentleness, nothing so gentle as real strength.
   Francis de Sales

2. Humility

Without humility there can be no humanity.
   John Buchan

A real test

The first real test of a really great man is his humility.
   John Ruskin

Helping others

A modest stillness

In peace there's nothing so becomes a man
As modest stillness and humility.
   William Shakespeare, *Henry V*, III.i.1

Too humble

Too humble, is half proud.
   Hanan J. Ayalti

Humility is ...

Humility is to make the right estimate of oneself.
   C.H. Spurgeon

3. Care over little things

Be great in little things.
   Augustine of Hippo

Attention to details

Attention to little things is a great thing.
   John Chrysostom

Doing the little I can do

I am only one. I can't do everything, but that won't stop me from doing the little I can do.
   Everest Hale

Being helpful

Cries for help

Every obnoxious act is a cry for help.
    Zig Ziglar

Other people's problems

You cannot teach a man anything; you can only help him to find it for himself.
    Galileo

Other people's monkeys

Dr Kenneth Blanchard, co-author of *One-Minute Manager*, warns against helping people too much by caring for and feeding their monkeys! He means that it not helpful to take on somebody else's problems (monkeys) as that only burdens you until you yourself collapse under the weight of these problems.

So 'helping' people with problems is talking with them and showing how *they* can solve their problems. It is not helpful to remove their problems for them.

Hospitality

If a man be gracious to strangers it shows that he is a citizen of the world and that his heart is no island, cut off from other islands, but a continent that joins them.
    Francis Bacon

To welcome a fellow man is to welcome the Shekhinah [divine presence].
    Jewish proverb

Mutual help

The human race would perish did they cease to aid each other. We cannot exist without mutual help. All therefore that need aid have a right to ask it of their fellow-men; and only one who has not the power to grant it can refuse without guilt.
    Walter Scott

> **Poet's corner**
>
> It is a kingly task, believe me, to help the afflicted.
>   Ovid

Be a carer

Assuredly nobody will care for him who cares for nobody.
   Thomas Jefferson

Everyone can be a carer

No one is useless in the world who lightens the burden of it for anyone else.
   Charles Dickens

Action

He who desires but acts not breeds pestilence.
He who would do good to another must do it in minute particulars.
   William Blake

Knowing ... being willing ... doing

Knowing is not enough; we must apply. Willing is not enough; we must do.
   Goethe

Being helpful

Be an encourager

Applaud

When someone does something well, applaud! You will make two people happy.

Samuel Goldwyn

Praise your children

Love your children with all your hearts, love them enough to discipline them before it is too late. Praise them for important things, even if you have to stretch them a bit. Praise them a lot. They live on it like bread and butter and they need it more than bread and butter.

Lavina Christensen Fugal, on being chosen 'Mother of the Year'

How to praise

> In the deserts of the heart
> Let the healing fountains start,
> In the prison of his days,
> Teach the free man how to praise.

'In Memory of W.B. Yeats' – lines inscribed on Auden's stone in Poets' Corner, Westminster Abbey

So says the president

The pat on the back, the arm around the shoulder, the praise for what was done right and the sympathetic nod for what wasn't are as much a part of golf as life itself.

Gerald R. Ford, at the dedication of the World Golf Hall of Fame, Pinehurst

Praise and flattery

Many men know how to flatter, few men know how to praise.

Edith Sitwell

Helping others

The aim of flattery

The aim of flattery is to soothe and encourage us by assuring us of the truth of an opinion we have already formed about ourselves.

The really great person

The really great person is the person who makes every one else feel great.
   G.K. Chesterton

Henry Ford

Henry Ford (1863–1947), born near Dearborn, Michigan, was an American industrialist without equal. After starting work as a machinist, and becoming chief engineer at Thomas Edison's Edison Illuminating Co., he went on to found the Ford Motor Company in 1903. Although he was not the first to invent an automobile, Ford was the first to make use of assembly lines – allowing cars to be mass produced at affordable prices. Over 15 million of his original 'Model T' cars were sold, and the industry he created has had a pronounced effect on the face of the planet.

At the age of 33 Henry Ford had one great idea in his mind – how to create a carriage that was propelled by petrol and not drawn by a horse. In 1896 Ford found many people who poured scorn on his idea. He became depressed until he met the inventor Thomas Edison at a conference. Henry Ford shared his dream with Edison, who replied, 'A self-contained unit that carries its own fuel. That's the thing! Keep at it!'

The Ford Motor Company may never have come into being without that timely piece of encouragement.

Concluding thought

I can live for two months on a good compliment.
   Mark Twain

Teamwork

Motivation principles

Certain principles have been pinpointed in businesses which make them better as a team. They are sometimes referred to as 'motivation' principles.

1. Involve people

Employers as well as employees, management as well as unions, now admit that everyone should be involved when changes are made, and decisions are taken.

2. Remove 'demotivators'

In common language this might be called getting rid of difficulties. If management knows what irritates employees and do nothing about it, they only have themselves to blame when things go wrong.

3. Pay the right salaries

Keeping wages as low as possible has not always been seen to be a sound business practice.

Henry Ford's five dollars a day

In 1914, when industrial workers were averaging about eleven dollars a week, Ford announced that his employees would be paid five dollars for an eight-hour day. His purpose was not only to motivate his workers to endure the drudgery of the assembly line but to bring his automobiles within their economic reach.

4. Be seen to be fair

This sometimes goes under the name of *equity*.
What's right for the bosses is also right for the workers.

5. Making it happen

These are reinforcement procedures which encourage feedback, and guide employees into carrying out tasks which management require.

6. Give rewards

Rewards or prizes should not be confined to children's parties. They act as positive incentives to people at work, whose daily lives may be very boring.

7. Set goals

In a smooth running business, employees will be as concerned to achieve goals as much as employers. But if there is not meaningful discussion about setting realistic goals there will never be convergence of interest in such matters.

Make sure all goals are achievable.

We need each other

The great cannot exist without the less, nor the less without the great.
Clement of Rome

Orchestras need second violins

It needs more skill than I can tell
To play the second violin well.
C.H. Spurgeon

Spreading a little happiness

Caring

People don't care how much you know, until they know how much you care – about them.
　Zig Ziglar

Rendering service

Consciously or unconsciously, every one of us does render some service or other. If we cultivate the habit of doing this service deliberately, our desire for service will steadily grow stronger, and will make, not only our own happiness, but that of the world at large.
　Gandhi

War and peace

You don't have to have fought in a war to love peace.
　Geraldine Ferraro

Using strength

Greatness lies not in being strong but in the right use of strength.
　Henry Ward Beecher

A candle

A happy man or woman is a radiant focus of good will, and their entrance into a room is as though another candle had been lighted.
　Robert Louis Stevenson

If I can stop one heart from breaking

> If I can stop one heart from breaking,
> I shall not live in vain;
> If I can ease one life the aching,
> Or cool one pain,
> Or help one fainting robin
> Upon his nest again,
> I shall not live in vain.
> Emily Dickinson

> **Poet's corner**
>
> The greatest pleasure I know is to do a good action by stealth, and to have it found out by accident.
>   Charles Lamb

Sympathy is ...

Sympathy is your pain in my heart.
    Author unknown

Sympathy is a divine passion

Next to love, sympathy is the divinest passion of the human heart.
    Edmund Burke

Sympathy for a toad

This is the first time I've actually held a toad. And my sympathy goes very much to the toad.
    Lord Skelmersdale (Roger Bootle-Wildraham), Undersecretary of the Environment in the British government, on opening a tunnel under a motorway to protect migrating toads

> **So says the president**
>
> ## The dream of the United Nations
>
> As caring, peaceful peoples, think what a powerful force for good we could be. Distinguished delegates, let us regain the dream the United Nations once dreamed.
>   Ronald Reagan, to the General Assembly of the United Nations, 1983

Spreading a little happiness

Uncommon graces

1. Gratitude

No shoes – no feet
Have mercy on me, O Beneficent One, for I was angry that I had no shoes – and then I met a man who had no feet.
    Chinese proverb

Fallen asleep
The person who has stopped being thankful has fallen asleep in life.
    Robert Louis Stevenson

2. Courtesy

Courteous to strangers
If a man be gracious and courteous to strangers, it shows he is a citizen of the world.
    Francis Bacon, *Essays, Of Goodness*

The cost of civility
Civility costs nothing.
    Author unknown

One day at a time
Anyone can carry his burden for one day.
Anyone can be pleasant, courteous and friendly for one day.
And that continued is all there is to life.
    Author unknown

3. Be straightforward

Don't try to be subtle in communicating
If you have an important point to make, don't try to be subtle or clever. Use a pile driver. Hit the point once. Then come back and hit it again. Then hit it a third time – a tremendous whack.
    Winston Churchill

Solving problems

Help from eleven words
Every problem contains within itself the seeds of its own solution.

Anticipating problems
Some problems can be solved by anticipating them. Then they don't even become problems.

Details
People too involved in details usually become unable to deal with great matters.
   La Rochefoucauld, *Maxims*

Causing confusion
   The centipede was happy quite,
   Until the toad in fun
   Said 'Pray, which leg goes after which?'
   Which worked her mind to such a pitch,
   She lay distracted in a ditch,
   Considering how to run.
   Author unknown

Coping with retirement

Keys to coping with retirement

1. Look ahead to retirement. On the day that you retire, the average person has 9,000 days to enjoy.
2. Make sure your affairs are in order. That way, you will have peace of mind.
3. Keep up with old friends, make new friends.

   You can make more friends in two months by becoming interested in other people than you can in two years by trying to get other people interested in you.
   Dale Carnegie

4. Develop relationships with your grandchildren.
5. Keep physically active.
6. Keep mentally active.
7. Consider taking up a part-time job.
8. Consider joining in with some voluntary work.
9. Get out as much as possible.
10. Eat properly.

Stress and old age

When you know what causes stress in old age you can take the necessary positive steps to alleviate unnecessary worry.
Stress in old age is often caused by:
- living alone and being unable to look after oneself;
- living in a state of fear because of our violent society;
- being unable to do things which were once taken for granted, like crossing the road or filling in forms.

Loneliness

Loneliness is the most terrible poverty.
   Mother Teresa

Going to sleep

Dos and don'ts for people with sleeping problems

DOs
1. Take some physical exercise during the day.
2. Make sure that there is fresh air in your bedroom.
3. Read a bit from a book you enjoy.
4. Try drinking a soothing bedtime drink, for example, a malted drink or just hot milk if you can stand it.
5. Make sure that you have a comfortable bed. As many old beds eventually sag this may involve buying a new mattress and/or bed.
6. Relax in a hot bath before you go to bed.
7. Wear ear-plugs or install double glazing if noise from outside disturbs you.
8. Develop your own night-time routine. It might be going for a short walk, just cleaning your teeth, or reading in bed.
9. If you are in pain or depressed ask your doctor to treat you.

DON'TS
1. Don't worry! If you can't sleep, then get up and do something instead of lying there worrying. It's the worry that gets to you, not the lack of sleep.
2. Don't eat heavy evening meals.
3. Don't have excess alcohol or coffee at night.
4. Don't go to bed until you feel sleepy.
5. Don't take work to bed with you.

> The old idea of a composer suddenly having a terrific idea and sitting up all night to write it is nonsense. Night-time is for sleeping.
> **Benjamin Britten**

6. If you smoke, try not to smoke before going to bed.
7. Try to keep calm before going to bed. Watching horror films or thrillers late at night will not help you to sleep.
8. Try not to sleep during the day.
9. Make sure that you are not too hot or too cold in bed.

Serving others

What we have done

When the day of judgment comes, we shall not be asked what we have read, but what we have done.
    Thomas à Kempis

Close to home

Charity begins at home, and justice begins next door.
    Charles Dickens

It is easier to love humanity as a whole than to love one's neighbour.
    Eric Hoffer

No special call needed

We have a call to do good, as often as we have the power and the occasion.
    William Penn

Just going about

I read somewhere that this young man Jesus Christ went about doing good. But I just go about.
    Toyohiko Kagawa

Noble acts

We can do noble acts without ruling earth and sea.
    Aristotle

Comfort

In a picture I want to say something comforting.
    Vincent Van Gogh

A love letter

I am a little pencil in the hand of a writing God who is sending a love letter to the world.
   Mother Teresa

Helping others

We all have enough strength to bear the misfortune of others.
   La Rochefoucauld

Sacrificial service

In Taiwan, the 68-year-old Gladys Aylward died as she lived – sacrificially. The *London Evening Standard* reported this event under the headline, 'The Small Woman's Last Sacrifice', as she had become ill as a result of giving away most of her bedding.

One of the orphans she brought up on the Chinese mainland visited her just before Christmas and asked what the veteran missionary would like as a Christmas present. Gladys Aylward said that she would love to have a cotton quilt. This orphan later discovered that when the temperature dropped to 40 degrees below zero, Gladys had given away her extra blanket to an orphan and her mattress to her Chinese housemaid.

All her possessions in the world consisted of one worn-out blanket. She caught flu and a few days later died in her sleep of pneumonia.

Consoling

A trifle consoles us because a trifle upsets us.
   Blaise Pascal

Learning and teaching

The thought, not the speaker

Examine what is said, not him who speaks.
> Arab proverb

Learning from a fool

The greatest lesson in life is to know that even fools are right sometimes.
> Winston Churchill

Perplexity

Perplexity is the beginning of knowledge.
> Kahlil Gibran

Seeking out a wise man

A single conversation across the table with a wise man is worth a month's study of books.
> Chinese proverb

Staying young

You can stay young as long as you learn.
> Emily Dickinson

The teacher's task

The teacher's task is not to implant facts but to place the subject to be learned in front of the learner and, through sympathy, emotion, imagination and patience, to awaken in the learner the restless drive for answers and insights which enlarge the personal life and give it meaning.
> Nathan M. Pusey, President of Harvard University

Learning

Tell me and I'll forget.
Show me, and I may not remember.
Involve me, and I'll understand.
> Native American proverb

Don't stop learning

Anyone who stops learning is old, whether at 20 or 80. Anyone who keeps learning stays young. The greatest thing in life is to keep your mind young.
 Henry Ford

'Borrowing' thoughts

Our best thoughts come from others.
 Ralph Waldo Emerson

Knowing enough

They know enough who know how to learn.
 Henry Adams

A lifelong habit

Unless we accept lifelong learning as a habit, we're shortening our lives.
 Author unknown

If a person's education is finished, he or she is finished.
 E.A. Filene

Playing and learning

You can do anything with children if you only play with them.
 Bismark

Winning allegiance

Let me teach for a generation, and I will become ruler of the state.
 Napoleon

Clever devils

Educate people without religion and you make them but clever devils.
 Duke of Wellington

Kindness

Acts of kindness

That best portion of a good man's life: his little, nameless, unremembered acts of kindness and of love.
    William Wordsworth

Kind words

Kind words can be short and easy to speak, but their echoes are truly endless.
    Mother Teresa

Give your time

You must give time to your fellow men – even if it's a little thing, do something for others, something for which you get no pay but the privilege of doing it.
    Albert Schweitzer

One kind word

One kind word can warm three winter months.
    Japanese proverb

To love and to help

After the verb 'to love', the verb 'to help' is the most beautiful verb in the world.
    Bertha von Suttner

Helping a friend

A person who seeks help for a friend, while needy himself, will be answered first.
    The Talmud

Tact

Tact is, after all, a kind of mind reading.
    Sarah Orne Jewett

The language of kindness

Kindness is a language the blind can see and the deaf can hear.
   Author unknown

Kind words

Kind words bring life, but cruel words crush your spirit.
   Proverbs 15:4

Like a wildfire

When you are kind to someone in trouble, you hope they'll remember and be kind to someone else. And it'll become like a wildfire.
   Whoopi Goldberg

Head and heart

To handle yourself ... use your head. To handle others ... use your heart.

Unkind people

Be kind to unkind people – they need it the most.
   Anonymous

April Fleming

In her mid-teens, April Fleming, an American schoolgirl, was dying of a blood disorder called polycythemia vera. In 1994 an American organization called Make-a-Wish Foundation asked April to make a wish which they would grant for her. To their surprise, instead of asking for a treat for herself, April asked the Foundation to buy Christmas presents for homeless children. Around America, people heard of April's wish, and sent gifts and donations which she used to make gift parcels for homeless people in Olympia, Washington. She died at the age of 17. Her wish was that 'everyone practise a random act of kindness to help a fellow human being who is in need'.

Great love

We can do no great things, only small things with great love.
   Mother Teresa

Giving versus getting

Giving away love

The love we give away is the only love we keep.
    Elbert Hubbard

How giving benefits the giver

Shared joy is a double joy;
shared sorrow is half a sorrow.
    Swedish proverb

We make a living by what we get,
but we make a life by what we give.
    Winston Churchill

Nothing is really ours until we share it.
    C.S. Lewis

The hand that gives, gathers.
    Proverb

Who shuts his hand has lost his gold.
Who opens it hath it twice told.
    George Herbert

Abundant giving brings abundant living.
    Proverb

Be generous, and you will be prosperous.
    Proverbs 11:25

Everyone has something to give

No man is so poor as to have nothing worth giving.
    Henry Wadsworth Longfellow

The more we give, the more we get

When the millionaire Percy Ross was six he went from house to house selling eggs. He refers to this experience as his first selling job. His father told him to give his customers an extra egg from time to time. He discovered that his customers reacted as if he had given them an extra dozen eggs. He never forgot the advice: always give to your customers.

Buying a Mercedes car

Some Mercedes car dealers arrange for a beautiful bouquet of flowers to be placed in the boot of each car they sell to a woman.

Giving money

Giving money is a very good criterion of a person's mental health. Generous people are rarely mentally ill people.
 Dr Karl A. Menninger

We made giving exciting

It went beyond idealism and that ridiculous term *activism*, which basically means talking about something but doing nothing! We made giving exciting.
 Bob Geldof, on organizing fund-raising concerts for famine relief in Africa

So says the president

And so, my fellow Americans, ask not what your country can do for you; ask what you can do for your country.
 J.F. Kennedy, Inaugural Address, 20 January 1961

Concluding thought

It is more blessed to give than to receive.
 Acts 20:35 (*AV*)

Showing love

Living with difficult people

It is no great matter to associate with the good and gentle, for this is naturally pleasing to all, and everyone happily enjoys peace, and loves those which do agree with him. But to be able to live in peace with hard and perverse persons is a great grace, and a most commendable thing.

Thomas à Kempis

Belief, hope, love, practice

All things are possible to him who believes, yet more to him who hopes, more still to him who loves, and most of all to him who practises and perseveres in these three virtues.

Brother Lawrence

A proverb to ponder

Love begets love.

Latin proverb

Something beautiful for God

To show great love for God and our neighbour, we need not do great things. It is how much love we put in the doing that makes our offering something beautiful for God.

Mother Teresa

To love another person ...

To love another person is to help them love God.

Søren Kierkegaard